BRIDGE FOR BE

A Step-By-Step Guide to Bidding, Play, Scoring, Conventions, and Strategies to Win

By: Game Nest

gamenest.org

This book is dedicated to all Bridge lovers across the globe.

If you enjoy the book, please consider leaving a review wherever you bought it.

Get All Our New Releases For FREE!

Sign up to our VIP Newsletter to get all of our future releases absolutely free!

www.gamenest.org/free

Contents

Introduction

Do you like activities that can provide hours of entertainment and also stimulate your mind? Do you enjoy solving puzzles? Do you like challenging and friendly competition? If the answer to each of these questions is yes, then you will certainly enjoy the card game known as Bridge.

Some people mistakenly think that Bridge is a simple game played only by the elderly on Sunday afternoons while drinking tea; the reality is quite different. I first learned to play Bridge while attending a Big Ten university, playing against fellow students who went on to have successful professional careers in engineering, medicine, law, academia, sports, and business. In fact, for nearly one hundred years, Bridge has been one of the most popular card games worldwide—for people of all ages. Every year, hundreds of professional Bridge tournaments are held during which players compete for money and other prizes, as well as for the prestige of being considered the very best at the game.

Unlike many simpler card games, success at Bridge is based on more than just luck. It requires knowledge, careful thought, memory, reasoning, planning, concentration, and teamwork. Really, the unique combination of luck, skill, and teamwork is part of what makes playing Bridge such an enjoyable pastime. Every hand you are dealt and every game you play presents a unique set of circumstances that you must navigate through based on your knowledge and experience.

Bridge is also a game that can be learned by just about anyone. When you first start playing—like when you first learned to ride a bicycle—you will feel uncertain and unsteady. But with knowledge, practice, and experience, you will become proficient at the game. Will you ever know everything there is to know about Bridge? Probably not. No one ever does. And that is part of the beauty of the game. No matter how much you already know, every hand of Bridge will present you with an opportunity to learn something new.

Bridge can also be an important social experience. It can open doors to meeting new, like-minded people, strengthen existing friendships, and teach you about the importance of cooperation, effective communication, taking risks, and building trust.

This book will introduce you to the game of Bridge. You will learn how the game works, the basic rules of play, and important terminology, as well as some more advanced aspects of the game, such as tactics and strategy.

Chapter 1:
The Basics of the Game

Bridge is a card game played by four people, no more and no less. It is played with a standard deck of fifty-two playing cards (no jokers)—the same type of cards used for card games such as Canasta, Pinochle, Poker, and Go Fish. The four players are divided into teams of two each, and the members of each team are referred to as partners. The four players are seated around a table (usually one with four sides), with partners directly facing each other (see diagram):

North
♠ 8 3 2
♥ K Q 8 7
♦ J 5
♣ A 9 6 5

West
♠ J 10 3
♥ A 6 3
♦ Q 8 7
♣ Q J 7 3

East
♠ A Q 7 6
♥ J 10 2
♦ 10 8 6
♣ 10 8 4

South
♠ K 9 5
♥ 9 5 4 2
♦ A K 9 4
♣ K 2

For the sake of clarity in discussions of any specific Bridge game, players are often referred to by their relative positions around the table and designated as North-South and East-West. So, North and South are partners and East and West are partners. And for any hand of Bridge being discussed, the dealer is always designated as South.

A standard deck of fifty-two cards has several important characteristics that are especially important for playing Bridge.

The deck includes four different **suits**, which are represented by symbols throughout this book: **spades** are represented by ♠, **hearts** by ♥, **diamonds** by ♦, and **clubs** by ♣.

Within each suit, there are thirteen cards with different **pips** or values. The pips are ace, king, queen, jack, ten, nine, eight, seven, six, five, four, three, and two, and they are arranged in a hierarchy of values, or ranks, with the ace of each suit being the highest-ranking card in that suit, followed by the king, queen, jack, ten, nine, eight, seven, six, five, four, three, and two, in that order.

In Bridge, the four suits are also arranged in a hierarchy of values, or ranking, with spades being highest, then hearts, then diamonds, and then clubs. An easy way to remember this ranking is that it goes in reverse alphabetical order: spades, hearts, diamonds, and clubs (SHDC). The two highest-ranking suits (spades and hearts) are referred to as the **major suits**, while the two lowest-ranking suits (diamonds and clubs) are called **minor suits**.

Bridge play is also divided into **hands, games**, and **rubbers**.

A hand of Bridge can be divided into four stages: the deal, the auction, the gameplay, and the scoring. Basically, the four stages are as follows: (1) all fifty-two cards are dealt out to the four players, so that each player ends up with thirteen cards; (2) the two teams engage in a process of verbal and competitive bidding, the end result being a commitment or **contract** by one of the two teams to win a certain number of **tricks**; (3) the gameplay then follows, during which the success or failure of the contract will be determined; (4) the points earned by either team are recorded. Each of these stages will be discussed in more detail in later chapters of this book.

During a Bridge hand, one particular suit (e.g., hearts) may be designated as the **trump** suit. This would mean that, for the duration of that hand, hearts are the highest-ranking suit in the deck. In other words, any card in that suit will "trump" (or win out over) even the highest cards in any other suit. For example, if hearts is the trump suit, and the two of hearts is played on an ace of spades, the player playing the two of hearts would win that trick, unless they are **overtrumped** by a higher-value trump card (e.g., the ten of hearts). For the next hand, the trump suit may be completely different, or there may be no trump suit at all.

A single game of bridge may require several hands be dealt and played out before a game is completed, or won. However, a rubber is always made up of at least two games, and no more than three.

A game is over when one team reaches one hundred points for that game, no matter how many hands it takes for that to happen. You can earn points in many different ways, but two important points are **offensive points** and **defensive points**. Only offensive points count toward winning a game; they can be earned by declaring during the bidding to accomplish a specific goal (e.g., winning a certain number of tricks), and then achieving that goal. On the other hand, if your opponents make a promise to win a certain number of tricks and your team is successful in preventing them from achieving that goal, you can earn defensive points.

A rubber is completed when one team has won two games, even if the other team hasn't won any. Of course, if each team wins a game, then a third game is played. A Bridge rubber, however, is not won by "winning two out of three games." The actual champion of a Bridge rubber is the team with the most points scored (for any reason) during the three (or two) games, regardless of how many games they won. In other words, a team might win two games but lose the rubber because they scored fewer total points than the other team.

How to Use This Book

I strongly recommend that you **not** try to read this entire book in one sitting. It will be too much information for you to absorb all at once. If you have zero experience with Bridge, you should probably read this section, and the glossary several times before you go any further.

If you are knowledgeable at playing other card games, you may catch on more quickly. For example, if you have played games like Hearts, Spades, Pinochle, or Whist, you will already be familiar with the relative ranking of cards and the concept of tricks. But if you have never touched playing cards before, it may take a bit longer to learn Bridge.

A good way to start is to use this book as your reference guide, your tutor, and your trusted friend, and to keep it beside you as you watch a few games of Bridge being played. As is the case with learning anything new, the best way to learn is to just do it. You will learn Bridge best by playing, and play as much as you can. Although it might be a tempting idea to start out by playing with a partner and opponents who are likewise inexperienced at Bridge, this may not be the best way to learn. When I first started learning how to play Bridge, I was fortunate to have someone as my regular partner and mentor who was not only an experienced and very good player, but also someone who had patience, good communication skills, a willingness to explain things carefully, and a recognition of my sincerity in wanting to learn not only to play, but also play at a high level.

Personal computers, mobile devices and apps, and the Internet now also provide many new opportunities for learning how to play Bridge. No longer do you need to be able to round up three other players who have a few free hours to play. You can now play with and/or against other players online, or even against the computer, and learn as you play. The best part about playing against the computer or on your mobile phone or tablet is that you can play at your own pace and will not need to feel like you are letting anyone down if you make a mistake or two. Just keep this book nearby as a reference while you play and you will do fine.

Once you have absorbed the basics and played your first game of Bridge, it will become easier. The key is to take each aspect of the game slowly and make sure you understand basic principles well before moving up to another level of play.

Chapter 2:
Playing a Hand of Bridge

In this chapter, you will learn how to play a single hand of Bridge: how the cards are dealt, the fundamentals of bidding for a contract, the mechanics of gameplay, and the basics of scoring.

The Deal

In Bridge, players take turns serving as the dealer. As with other card games, the dealer is the person who shuffles and distributes the cards to all of the players at the table so that the playing of the game can begin. To determine who will be the first dealer, cards are drawn from a shuffled deck. More specifically, a player volunteers to shuffle the cards. The stack of shuffled cards is then placed facedown in the center of the table. Then, starting with the player immediately to the left of the shuffler, each player selects a card from the top of the stack. After all four players have selected a card, the drawn cards are compared, and the player with the highest-ranking card (according to the suit and Pip rankings discussed in Chapter 1) is designated as the first dealer.

Then, before cards are dealt, the player to the left of the now-selected dealer **cuts** the cards.

At this point, all fifty-two cards are dealt (one at time) to each player in a clockwise direction, starting with the player to the left of the dealer, and ending with the dealer. At the end of the deal, each player should have thirteen cards. It is an important part of Bridge etiquette to not pick up and look at any of your cards until the entire **deal** is completed. Once the deal is completed, it is customary for each player to count the cards they have been given to make sure they have thirteen of them. If any player discovers that they have more or less than thirteen cards, a **misdeal** is called. When this happens, all of the cards are collected by the original dealer, reassembled into the deck, and passed to the player to the left of the original dealer, who now shuffles the cards and deals again. The players take turns dealing the cards for each hand played, with the deal rotating to the left of the previous dealer, and so on.

After you receive your cards, you should carefully organize them in your hands. It is customary to sort them into suits, and then, within each suit, organize them highest to lowest in terms of card value. Typically, the suits are also arranged from left to right:

spades, hearts, clubs, and diamonds. However, for reasons which we will discuss later, that may not always be a good idea.

The Auction

Once the deal has been successfully completed, and players have carefully examined the group of cards they have been dealt, the hand then moves into the **auction** phase. During this phase, the two teams engage in a round of competitive verbal bidding; the basic goal is for one of the two teams to establish or win the contract, which will then guide play during the playing of the hand.

Bidding for the Contract

Starting with the dealer, and then moving to the left, the players take turns stating their **bid** (if any) out loud. Players are not obligated to bid, and if they choose not to bid, they say the word **pass**. Bidding is part of the language of Bridge, and bids serve at least two purposes.

First, a bid is a proposal to all of the other players as to what you believe your team can accomplish during the playing of the hand. More specifically, by bidding, you are proposing how many tricks you believe you and your partner can win, with a particular

17

suit as the trump suit, during the play phase of the hand. It is also acceptable to propose a contract with "no" trump suit specified, or a **no-trump** contract. This means that during play there will be no trump suit cards that can override the value of cards in other suits.

Basically, a player bids by declaring a number and a suit (spades (♠), hearts (♥), diamonds (♦), clubs (♣), or no-trump.).

Examples of possible "bids" are "two clubs," "three hearts," "three diamonds," or "two no-trump."

In addition to proposing a contract, a bid also serves as a way of providing information to your partner regarding important characteristics of the set of thirteen cards you have been dealt. Don't worry, relaying or communicating information about the cards you are holding in this way is not cheating. In fact, as you shall learn in later chapters, communication between partners in this manner is an essential part of the game of Bridge. However, all other communication during bidding is strictly forbidden, as are gestures and other means of conveying pleasure or displeasure with your cards or your partner's bids. The integrity of the game requires you to declare all of your bids in an even tone and without undue inflection or emphasis. The proper expression of a bid of 1 ♣ would simply be "one club." If you were to hesitate or express your uncertainty by saying something like, "I think I'm going to bid a club," then you would be conveying improper information to your partner.

As stated earlier, the dealer always makes the first bid. Each player has the option to pass on their turn if they determine that their hand is not a good one, or if, for some other reason, they no longer wish to attempt to win the contract.

Another important rule is that all bids must be made according to the hierarchy of suits mentioned earlier, lowest to highest: clubs, diamonds, hearts, spades, and, finally, no-trump. And, as you can see in the bidding ladder diagram below, the lowest bid possible is one club and the maximum possible bid is 7 no-trump. The first person to bid can start the auction with a bid of one club or higher. Each following bidder must then make a bid that is to the right and higher on the bidding ladder, or pass.

7♣ 7♦ 7♥ 7♠ 7NT

6♣ 6♦ 6♥ 6♠ 6NT

5♣ 5♦ 5♥ 5♠ 5NT

4♣ 4♦ 4♥ 4♠ 4NT

3♣ 3♦ 3♥ 3♠ 3NT

2♣ 2♦ 2♥ 2♠ 2NT

1♣ 1♦ 1♥ 1♠ 1NT

So, for example, if a player opens the bidding with one diamond, subsequent bids can only be those options to the right and above one diamond (e.g., one heart, two clubs, two spades, four hearts, etc.).

Deciding whether or not to bid, what to bid, how many tricks you will propose to win, when to pass, and how to interpret and respond to the bids of your opponents during the auction, are all very important topics that will be discussed in much more detail in later chapters.

The auction proceeds clockwise until it is ended by three consecutive players saying pass. At this point, the last bid or proposed contract becomes the official contract that will guide the play phase of the hand, and the first player to have offered a bid in that suit (or no-trump) becomes the **declarer**, and the opposing team becomes the **defenders**. The team that wins the auction is now contracted to win the number of tricks they last proposed during the auction.

So, for example, if the bidding went as follows:

South - pass

West - one spade

North - pass

East - two spades

South - pass

West - four spades

North - pass

Fast - pass

South - pass

The auction has ended because three consecutive players said pass (North, East, and South), and the contract has been won by East-West at four spades.

West, who was the first to bid spades, becomes the declarer, while North-South become the defenders. It is now the obligation of East-West to complete their four-spade contract, and it is the goal of the defenders to prevent that from happening.

If all four players pass on their first turn in the auction, that is called a **pass out**. In this instance, the cards are collected, reassembled into the deck, and passed to the player to the left of the previous dealer, who then shuffles them and deals them again.

Doubling and Redoubling

If the team that wins the auction fails to fulfill their contract, they will be penalized in the scoring, and the defenders will earn defensive points. If you (or your partner) believe that the other team has bid too high, you (or your partner) can use your turn during the auction to issue a verbal challenge rather than offer a bid. You accomplish this by saying the word **double**. This declaration communicates the belief that the opposing team can be prevented from fulfilling their contract. If you are right, then the defensive points your team will receive for the contracting team's failure will literally be doubled. However, if the contract is fulfilled, then the contracting team's offensive points are doubled. Also, if—in spite of your double—the contracting team still believes that they can fulfill the contract, either member of that team can say **redouble** when it is their turn to bid again. If they end up fulfilling the contract, the offensive points they would normally earn for completing their contract are then multiplied by four. In other words, the double is doubled.

There are certain circumstances under which doubling is a much riskier move and is therefore usually a bad idea. If your opponents' contract is only for a partial score toward a game (e.g., two hearts or three diamonds), doubling is usually not worth the risk because if they are successful, the doubling of their offensive points would also win them the game. An even riskier situation is if your failed double not only wins your opponents the game, but also the rubber. This can happen if they are winning their second game. It can also happen if, even though they are only winning their first game, they will score so many defensive points from your failed doubling (or their redoubling) that even though you might have won the other two games, they will win the rubber on total points. In such situations, the potential benefit of doubling if you are right is clearly not worth the risk of being wrong.

On the other hand, if you are already down one game and your opponents seem to be headed for a contract that could win them the second game, there would usually be no significant risk in doubling—unless you are already way ahead on points from penalties the opponents have previously incurred. Although your chances for success may not be good, you might get lucky.

Another important note to consider is that doubling or redoubling does not bring the auction to an end. Even if a bid is doubled or redoubled, another player can still offer another contract bid. For example, if a player bids four hearts and the next opponent doubles, the original bidder's partner can then bid four spades. This is also true after a redouble, although that is rarely done.

Also, sometimes a double issued in the first round of bidding is not a comment on the likelihood of a contract being fulfilled (**penalty double**), but rather a tactic called a **takeout double**. When one player bids a suit and the player in the next seat says "double," the doubler is asking his/her partner to bid at the next possible level in their best suit.

Playing the Hand

The play phase of a hand of Bridge proceeds as follows. The person (from the opposing team) to the left of the declarer makes the opening **lead** by selecting a card from those they have been dealt and laying it faceup in the middle of the table. There are many different factors that might be considered in choosing which card to lead with, and those factors will be discussed in later chapters of this book. Furthermore, once a card is exposed by any player so that it's face can be seen by other players, it is considered played, even if it has not yet been placed faceup on the table. And a card cannot be withdrawn once it has been played, except under very unusual circumstances.

Then—and not before—the declarer's partner, now referred to as the **dummy**, places their cards faceup on the table. The cards are arranged in four vertical rows by suit (highest to lowest), with the highest-value card in each suit at the top of each row closest to the dummy player, and the lowest-value card at the bottom of each row closest to the declarer. It is also customary to place the trump suit in the leftmost row, in this case spades, from the perspective of the declarer. See diagram.

A♠	4♥	J♣	K♦
J♠		9♣	Q♦
9♠		8♣	10♦
2♠			5♦
			3♦

At this point, the dummy player becomes just an observer of the play while their partner, the declarer, plays the cards from both their own hand and the dummy hand at the appropriate time.

The declarer then chooses a card from the dummy to play, and places it faceup on top of the already-played card. If the declarer touches a card in the dummy's possession, it is deemed as played, unless the declarer is simply rearranging the dummy's cards. Some players prefer to verbally state which card they will play from the dummy before actually doing so; once it has been named, it must be played.

Moreover, the card chosen and played from the dummy must meet certain conditions.

First, if possible, this card must match the suit of the card originally played (when there are cards of that suit in the dummy's possession). And the declarer can choose any card from that suit to play. If there are no cards of that suit in the dummy's possession, then the declarer can play any card they want, including a trump card.

At this point, the player from the opposing team, to the right of the declarer, must choose a card from their hand to play. This card must also match (or follow) the suit of the first card played, when possible. If it is not possible to follow suit, the card played could be a trump card. Or, if the dummy played a trump card, it could be a higher-ranked trump card. Or, the player could play a card from some other suit, if the player has no cards in the original suit, or if—for some tactical reason—they choose not to play a higher-ranked trump card.

Finally, the declarer must choose a card from their hand to play on the three cards already played and place it faceup on top of the stack of cards. The declarer is bound by the same rules that governed the choice of cards played by the other players. Specifically, the card must match the suit of the first-played card (if possible). Or, It can be a trump card or a higher-ranked trump card, or a card from some other suit, if there are no cards of the original suit in the declarer's hand.

The four cards that have now been played and are now on the table constitute a trick. In other words, a trick consists of four cards, one from each player's hand, played in a clockwise order. The winner of the trick is the player who played the highest-ranking card of that suit or the highest-ranking trump card. For example, if the cards played are the ace of clubs, the two of clubs, the six of clubs, and the three of clubs, the player that played the ace of clubs wins the trick. But if one or more trump cards have been played on the trick, the player who played the highest-ranked trump card wins the trick. The player who wins the trick collects the four cards and stacks them on top of each other, facedown, on the table in front of him/her. If the trick has been won by the contracting team, it is always placed in front of the declarer. Tricks won by defenders are all kept together on the table in front of one of the defending team members.

The winner of the first trick then leads for next trick, and so on, until all thirteen tricks have been played and won.

At that point, the total number of tricks won by each team is counted. As discussed earlier, a team can **make** the contract by winning a number of tricks equal to (or higher than) the number they bid. If the contracting team ends up winning fewer tricks than the contract promised, then they have failed to make the contract. When a team fails in this way, it may be said by experienced Bridge players that they have been **set** (as in setback), or **went down** (as in went down in defeat).

If during the course of playing the hand, the declarer or either of the opponents believes that they have the cards necessary to win all of the remaining tricks (e.g., they have only trump cards remaining, and no other players have any trump cards), they may declare that openly. This is done largely as a means of saving time. They would then expose their remaining cards by laying them on the table in front of them. Their opponents may choose to either accept the **claim**, or reject it. If it is accepted, the hand is deemed completed and scored appropriately. If the claim is rejected, the play then continues with the declaring player's remaining cards still faceup on the table in front of them.

Scoring the Hand

When a team fulfills its contract, it scores a certain number of offensive points, depending on the type of contract and the trump suit, if any. For any contract, no offensive points are scored for the first six tricks won. Collectively, these first six tricks are called the **book**. So when a player offers a bid like two diamonds, what they are actually proposing is that they will win a total of eight tricks, or two plus the book. Similarly, a bid of four spades is actually a proposal to win a total of ten tricks, or four plus the book.

If the trump suit is a minor suit (clubs or diamonds), the team completing the contract scores 20 points per trick won above the book. For example, a completed contract of five clubs would score 100 points. Such a contract would also then win that game, since that team has now reached 100 points.

If the trump suit is a major suit (hearts or spades), the team completing the contract would score 30 points per trick won above the book. For example, a completed contract of four hearts would score 120 points. This successful contract would also win a game since the team has scored at least 100 points.

If there is no trump suit (i.e., it was a no-trump contract), the team completing the contract would score 40 points for the first trick won above the book and then score 30 points for each additional trick won above the book. For example, a completed contract of three no-trump would score 100 points and also win a game.

Contracts fulfilled may get you all the way to completed game (e.g., five diamonds), or they may not (e.g., three diamonds). When they do not, the game is called a **partial game**. It will then be necessary to play additional hands and complete additional contracts in order for either team to complete and win that game. Of course, even if a team has bid and completed a partial-game contract (e.g., three hearts), that game could still be won by the other team by bidding and completing a contract (e.g., four of spades) that finishes off the game on the next hand.

When a team wins more tricks than they promised, they have earned **overtricks**. For every trick won over the number promised in the contract the scoring is as follows: 20 additional offensive points are awarded per overtrick if the contract was in a minor suit; 30 additional offensive points are awarded per overtrick if the contract was in a major suit, or if it was a no-trump contract. However, these overtrick points do not count toward the winning of a game.

If a contracting team wins fewer tricks than it promised, their opponents score defensive points for each of the **undertricks**. The number of defensive points scored depends on a couple of factors: Has the team that failed to fulfill their contract completed any previous games? And was the contract doubled or redoubled?

When a team has already completed a previous game (toward a rubber) they are deemed **vulnerable**. When a vulnerable team fails to complete a contract successfully, their opponents get more defensive points than they would get if the unsuccessful team was not vulnerable. Specifically, when the unsuccessful team is **not vulnerable**, their opponents score 50 defensive points for every undertrick. But, if the unsuccessful team is vulnerable, the defensive points are doubled (100 points for every undertrick).

If the contract was doubled, and the contracting team is not vulnerable, their opponents score 100 defensive points for the first undertrick, 200 defensive points each for the second and third undertricks, and 300 defensive points for each additional undertrick. If the contract was doubled, and the contracting team is vulnerable, then their opponents score 200 defensive points for the first undertrick, 300 defensive points each for the second and third undertricks, and 300 defensive points for each additional undertrick.

Regardless of how defensive points are earned, they do not count toward winning a game, only toward winning the Rubber.

Finally, if a team's contract was doubled, and they are successful in completing that contract, then all of the offensive points they score are doubled. For example, if a team wins and fulfills a contract for four spades, and that contract is doubled, they would score 80 points per trick won, instead of the usual 40 points per trick. Points earned for overtricks would also be doubled. And if they redoubled, all of the offensive points won are multiplied by four.

Other Ways to Score Points

When a contract to win twelve tricks is completed successfully, that is called a **small slam**. A contract to win all thirteen Tricks, when successful, is called a **grand slam**. Because such achievements in Bridge are not only quite rare, but also quite difficult, bonus points are awarded for the completed slam contract as follows.

    a. Small slam - vulnerable - 500 points

    b. Small slam - not vulnerable - 750 points

    c. Grand slam - vulnerable - 1000 points

    d. Grand slam - not vulnerable - 1500 points

Another way bonus points can be earned is if the declarer's team succeeds on a doubled contract. If they do, they get a 50-point bonus. This is sometimes known as "50 for the insult." For making a redoubled contract, the bonus is 100 points.

For winning a rubber, a team also gets a bonus of 700 points if they won it two games to zero. If they won two games to one, the bonus is only 500 points.

Finally, the top five trumps (A K Q J 10) are called **honors**, and if one player holds all five of these cards, that player's team also scores a bonus of 150 points. If a player holds only four honors, their team gets a 100-point bonus. If there is no trump suit and a player holds all four aces, that player's team scores 150 bonus points for honors. Since there is no skill in scoring for honors, players sometimes agree to play without the honor bonuses.

33

The Scoresheet

The points won during bridge hands, games, and rubbers are typically recorded on a single piece of paper divided into two columns. These columns are headed by WE and THEY (representing the two teams), with a horizontal line partway down (see diagram below).

We	They
20	
50	
100	500
200	150
30	750
70	120
240	
60	120
Total 770	**1640**

Before the rubber starts, one player is designated as the scorekeeper. Points scored for tricks won as part of successful contracts are entered below the horizontal line on the paper, in that team's column. As noted earlier, these are the only points that count toward completing and winning a game.

Other points scored (e.g., bonuses, overtricks, honors, and defensive points) are placed above the horizontal line and do not count toward the completion or winning of a game. But they do count toward winning a rubber.

For the second and third games of the rubber, another horizontal line is drawn across the vertical line, and that then becomes the line below and above which the scoring for those games is recorded. And scoring for this game begins with each side at zero points for that game. In other words, no excess contract points from previous games carry over to the next game.

If, for some reason, the full rubber cannot be completed, and only one team has won a game, that team is given a 300-point bonus. A team with a partial score (e.g., they have completed a partial contract) is given a 100-point bonus.

Chapter 3:
The Auction

In this chapter, I will discuss the auction stage of a hand of Bridge in more detail, provide some important guidelines for bidding, and consider various factors that might influence a team's success or failure at completing their contract.

Competition for the Contract

Calling the bidding phase of a Bridge hand an auction is not arbitrary. A Bridge auction truly is a competition, not unlike an auction for art or antiques. Obviously, if you don't engage in the bidding process, you won't win that which is being auctioned, nor will you complete a Bridge contract or win a Bridge game or rubber. A Bridge auction, like any other auction, requires that you get involved and take some risks. I am sure that you have heard the expression, "nothing ventured, nothing gained." This is true in Bridge as well. Nevertheless, caution is also an entirely appropriate attitude during a Bridge auction.

Bidding during the auction phase of a Bridge hand is truly "gambling" in some respects. But it need not be reckless, irresponsible, and foolish gambling, like betting on a horse at a racetrack because his paddock number happens to also be your "lucky number." In Bridge, the choices you make always involve some risk, but you can minimize that risk by literally "having your head in the game." During any Bridge hand, game, or rubber, there is a lot of information immediately available to you, and this is information you can easily obtain through various legitimate means. This information can then be used to make more educated guesses about what may happen on any given hand.

Prior to the Bridge rubber even starting, you may know certain things about the other players in the game, including your own partner. For example, they may be relatively inexperienced at Bridge, or there may be certain characteristics of their personality (e.g., riskiness or competitiveness) that could be relevant to the gameplay. Even the mental state of one or more of the other players (e.g., fatigued, excited, bored, etc.) could prove to be important information.

Also, once the cards are dealt, the ones you receive can provide you with a lot of information—if you know what to look for and how to evaluate it. Even more information can be gained during the auction by listening carefully to the bids, counterbids, and even the passes of the other players, including your partner. Also, the expressions registered on your opponents' faces when they first look at their cards, how they hold or organize the cards in their hands, the tone of their voice or their vocal inflections when they bid or respond to other bids, can often be informative. Just as in Poker, some Bridge players may not have a very good "poker face" or may behave in ways that can help you identify what they are thinking.

Most importantly, in Bridge it is entirely acceptable—and an essential part of the game—for teammates to communicate valuable information between each other about the characteristics of the cards they hold, what contracts seem feasible, what card should be played next, and what can or cannot be done to counter the efforts of their opponents. This is acceptable as long as it is done indirectly, through bids made, passes, doubles, redoubles, cards led, played, or discarded, or other entirely legitimate means, and it is done openly so that both teams know and can interpret what is being said.

To Speak or Not

At various points, as the auction progresses around the table, you will have a turn to speak. Depending on where you are seated at the table, and what has happened previously, you will have the opportunity to make an **opening bid**, **overcall**, respond to an opening bid by your partner, respond to your partner's overcall, or pass.

Evaluating Your Cards

The most important factor for determining if you will bid, what your bid will be, and/or how you will respond to the bids and other actions of your partner and your opponents, is the **strength** of the cards you have been dealt. In Bridge, this strength is determined by several factors.

Face-card points (FCPs). Face cards are assigned points as follows: ace = 4; king = 3; queen = 2; jack = 1. So, if you are holding five face cards (e.g., two aces, one king, one queen, and one jack), you would have a total of 14 face card points. Each suit then has 10 possible face-card points (FCPs), and so the deck has 40 possible FCPs in total.

Suit length. The length of any suit is the number of cards of that suit you have been dealt. Points can then also be calculated based on this characteristic, thus contributing to the strength of your cards.

1. Five-card suit = 1 point

2. Six-card suit = 2 points

3. Seven-card suit = 3 points

4. Eight-card suit = 4 points

So, for example, if you also hold six hearts, you would add an additional 2 points to the 14 face-card points already calculated, giving you a total of 16 points. Similarly, if you have eight clubs in your hand, you would add an additional 4 points to the 14 face-card points, giving you a total of 18 points.

Short suits. If you have only a few cards (or no cards) in any suit, this can also be considered an important characteristic. You should add value points to your cards as follows:

1. Two cards in a suit (**doubleton**) = 1 point

2. One card in a suit (**singleton**) = 2 points

3. No cards in a suit (**void**) = 3 points

Collectively, the suit length and short suit characteristics of your cards are often referred to as **distribution**. For example, if you hold four spades, three hearts, three diamonds, and three clubs, your cards have **balance** because there is no truly "long" suit. In contrast, your thirteen cards might contain seven diamonds, two hearts, two spades, and two clubs. These cards are clearly unbalanced, with a very long diamond suit and three doubletons. Under some circumstances, it can be good to have cards with more balance between the suits. Under other circumstances, having one or two very long suits can be beneficial.

Here are some other examples of possible deals.

Your cards: ♠AK1064 ♥KJ6 ♦7 ♣Q854

You have 16 points: 4 points for the ace, 3 points each for the two kings, 2 points for the queen, 1 point for the jack, one point for the five-card spades suit, and 2 points for the singleton.

Your cards: ♠A9875 ♥98643 ♦73 ♣7

You have only 9 points: 4 points for the ace, 2 points for two five-card suits, 1 point for the doubleton, and 2 points for the singleton.

Your cards: ♠KJ954 ♥ — ♦KQ93 ♣A853

You have 13 FCPs, 1 point for a five-card suit, and the void is worth 3 points, which gives you a total of 17 points.

Your cards: ♠A1076 ♥865 ♦843 ♣742

These cards are worth only 4 points because of the ace.

Making an Opening Bid

Once you have evaluated your cards, you must then decide if you will bid or not. Certain wise bidding practices have been devised, based largely on experience with what is likely to happen during the play part of the game. For example, if the value of your hand is 12 points or less, this is your first opportunity to bid, and no one has bid before you, you should definitely pass. This is because, with so few points, your cards are not very strong. Experience has shown that the chances of winning enough tricks to complete a contract with so few points are not very good. So, bidding anything is not worth the risk. However, if your card value is at least 13 points, with at least 10 FCPs, you have a clear long suit (at least five cards), and your partner has not bid before you, then you should definitely bid something.

But what should you bid? There are many bidding **conventions** that you will want to learn in order to play bridge at an advanced level. These are too numerous and complex to be discussed here, but they will be covered in greater detail in later chapters. The most important thing to know about Bridge conventions at this point is that they are sets of rules previously agreed upon about what should be "bid" under certain circumstances. Furthermore, because they are conventions that most experienced Bridge players know about and follow, they also serve as a kind of language (or code) that Bridge partners can use to communicate with each other, without actually seeing each other's cards, or the cards of the other team. For example, if I pass on my first opportunity to bid, and no one has bid before me, I am not only passing up my turn, I am also telling my partner that I have less than 13 points in my hand. Why? Because they know I am also an experienced Bridge player who knows how to calculate the strength of my cards. When I pass, it is therefore reasonable for them to assume that I have correctly evaluated my cards and determined that they are worth less than 13 points, even if they have no idea of their exact value at this point. If both players on a team understand these rules and communicate effectively with each other by following them, they are much more likely to successfully complete contracts and are therefore also more likely to win at Bridge.

It is also true that when either you or your teammate makes the first bid during an auction, your team is at a distinct psychological advantage. You have already begun exchanging information with your partner, and so the risk to your opponents has slightly increased. Generally speaking, anything you can do to maximize your opponents' risk, while minimizing your own, is a wise strategy in Bridge.

Now, assume that you are the dealer and you have carefully evaluated your cards and they are telling you to bid something.

Here are some important guidelines to follow. If your cards are worth 13 to 21 points, and you have a five-plus-card major suit, you should open the bidding at the one level in that major suit (e. g., one spade). If you have 13 to 21 points, and a minor suit of least four cards, bid at the one level in that suit (e.g., one diamond). With three cards each in both minor suits, bid one club. With four or more cards in each minor suit, open the bidding with one diamond. You should only open with one no-trump if you have 16 to 18 points, balance (4-3-3-3, 4-4-3-2, or 5-3-3-2), and no five-card major suit.

Here are a few more examples to consider:

Your cards: ♠A1095 ♥KJ62 ♦Q84 ♣75

Although it's more fun to bid, you have only 11 points, so you should most certainly pass.

Your cards: ♠ K10752 ♥KJ962 ♦AJ6 ♣ -

You have 17 points total and 12 FCPs. You should open the bidding. And since your spades and hearts are equal in number, but you have more FCPs in hearts, an opening bid of one heart would be the best place to start.

Your cards: ♠KJ8732 ♥A98753 ♦- ♣5

While you do have 17 points total, 9 of them are length and short suit points. And you don't have 10 FCPs, so you should pass.

Opening at the Two Level

Under certain circumstances, in order to communicate to your partner that you have especially strong cards, it may also be appropriate to open the bidding at the two level. This is a very aggressive bid, usually reserved for situations where your cards are so strong that the success of your contract, even at the level needed to win a game, is extremely likely. However, opening at the two level can also be a type of defensive bidding, meant only to annoy your opponents or interfere with their bidding. The situations where opening at the two level would be appropriate will be discussed in more detail in future chapters.

Of course, opening the bidding does not guarantee that you will win the auction and have the opportunity to complete the contract, win a game, or even score any points at all. After your bid, your opponents will also have an opportunity to attempt to establish a contract that they might complete and to score some points and maybe even win the first game. That is why it's called competitive bidding. For example, if you have only 13 points, and are long in spades and short in clubs, it is possible that at least one of your opponents is long in clubs and short in spades. If that opponent also has the opportunity to bid immediately after you, and has enough points to open, they might respond to your bid of one spade by bidding two clubs. If your partner does not have many FCPs at all, and the opponent's partner likes the idea of playing for a contract in clubs, you will likely lose this contract opportunity to the other team. In the end, it will be the team that has the best cards, communicates most effectively, and is willing to take the highest calculated risk that will "win" the auction.

Responding to Your Partner

When your partner makes an opening bid, and the bidding comes back to you, you will need to decide how to respond to your partner. Your response will depend largely on the opening bid, and, of course, the strength of your cards. Assuming your partner has opened at one level in some suit, there are many different levels of card strength that you might have, and your response should be different in each situation.

Very Weak Cards

If your cards are worth 5 or fewer total points, don't even think about responding. You won't be much help your partner, no matter what suit your partner mentioned. You should pass.

Weak Cards

Six to 9 total points is a bit better, but it probably will still not help your partner much, especially if the points are on the low end (6 or 7). But if you also have at least three cards in your partner's opening suit, you likely have at least eight cards of that suit between the two of you. Under such circumstances, you should probably respond in some way. But how?

If the opening bid is in a minor suit (clubs or diamonds), a simple raise of your partner's opening bid would be acceptable (e.g., two clubs in response to one club). Or, if you have a four-card major suit, you could respond at the one level in that suit (e.g., one heart), especially if your point support is weak. This tells your partner three things: you have some support, but it isn't great, and your longest suit is hearts. If you have two four-card majors, always respond in hearts to keep the bidding as low as possible.

However, if you have no support for your partner's minor suit and no other suit you can bid at the one level, you should respond with one no-trump, even if your hand is not well-balanced.

If the opening bid is in a major suit, respond at the one level whenever possible. Otherwise, a simple raise of your partner's opening bid to confirm a trump fit would be acceptable (e.g., two hearts in response to one heart).

If your cards feature length in the suit mentioned by your partner (e.g., five or six) but are weak in points, another option is to respond at the four level. For example, your partner opens with one heart, and then you respond with four hearts. This is called a **double-jump to game**. It tells your partner that you have very good trump support and no balance, with at least one singleton or void.

If your partner opened with a bid of one no-trump, you should probably pass—unless you think two of some other suit would be a safer contract. If you bid two diamonds, two hearts, or two spades, this is called a **sign-off**; it essentially communicates to your partner that you don't think your team can do much better than a two-level contract in some suit so should stop right there. Your partner's response to you should then be to pass. And you should never bid two clubs in this situation because that has a much more specific meaning which will be discussed in another chapter.

Average Card Strength

If you have 10 to 12 points, with a four-plus-card suit, that will be good support for your partner at either the one or two Level. If the opening bid is one of a minor suit, stay at the one level, if possible. However, if the opening bid is one of a major suit, an acceptable response would be to bid two of a new major suit (e.g., two hearts in response to one spade) or two in a minor suit (e.g., two clubs).

Above-Average Card Strength

If you have between 13 and 15 points, and at least four cards in the suit bid, the appropriate way to respond to your partner's bid is with a **jump-raise.** The key message you are sending to your partner is, "Hey, between the two of us, I think our cards are strong enough to bid to a level at which we could win a game." For example, in response to an opening bid of one spade, you would respond with three spades.

On the other hand, to communicate that you have a balanced hand with no four-card major suits, a jump into no-trump (e.g., a bid of two no-trump in response to one spade), or even three no-trump, would be appropriate.

Strong Cards

With 16 to18 points, and a long and strong suit, a jump into a new minor suit communicates to your partner that you have a very good set of cards indeed. This is called a **jump-shift**. For example, a response of three clubs in response to an opening of one club would be acceptable. And a jump to three no-trump in response to one club would communicate not only very good card strength, but also a balanced hand. Notice here that a bid of three no-trump would also be a game-winning bid level, and the jump-shift in this example is just one of the ways you can get to a game-winning contract.

In response to your partner's opening bid of one no-trump, you could also respond with two no-trump; this is called an **invitation** bid, or an **invitation** to game. You are saying to your partner that you think your combined cards might be strong enough to succeed at a three no-trump level, and thus win a game. And, you are inviting your partner to respond with a bid of three no-trump if they agree.

However, a response of three of any major suit in response to your partner's one no-trump opening bid is called **forcing**, and basically says to your partner, "I don't think a no-trump contract is a good idea." You would prefer to search for a major suit fit, and if your partner has at least three cards in the suit you named, their response should be four in that suit. Otherwise, they will then bid three no-trump.

Excellent Cards

On rare occasions, when your partner has opened (and thus communicated that they are holding at least 13 points), it may be the case that your hand is even stronger (e.g., 19 to 22 points). Under such circumstances, completing a game-winning contract is very likely. In fact, between you and your partner, you hold nearly all of the FCPs in the entire deck. A jump-shift from one major suit into another is acceptable (e.g., a response of two spades after an opening bid of one heart). You may even want to begin thinking about working your way up to a contract of six of some suit (e.g., a small slam). In a later chapter, I will discuss in detail how best to explore that option and the risks involved.

Exceptional Cards

With a 23+ points, you should immediately be thinking about a grand-slam bid, even if your partner has average card strength. And you would let your partner know your thinking by jump-raising the game in some suit (e.g., four hearts or spades, or five diamonds or clubs. In fact, there are very specific and detailed conventions for exploring with your partner the possibility of playing for a grand-slam contract. These conventions will be discussed in more detail in a later chapter.

One final note about bidding. Anytime a player bids four of a major suit, or three no-trump, they are making a **sign-off** bid. In other words, the player is communicating to their partner to not bid up any further.

Overcalls

As discussed earlier, an overcall is when you counter a bid by your opponents with a bid of your own. Bidding when your opponents have already entered the bidding is always a higher-risk move. For the most part, decisions to overcall should be based on the nature of the cards you hold, as well as what you can learn about the cards of your partner and opponents during the auction. For example, if one of your opponents has opened, then you know that this player has cards worth at least 13 points, with at least 10 FCPs. If their partner responds, they probably have at least 6 FCPs, giving that team at least 16 FCPs, and perhaps as many as 19 FCPs. That is nearly half of all of the FCPs in the deck. This means that, at best, you and your partner could have as many as 24. But it is more likely you only have around 20 FCPs. And so, while it is worth exploring the possibility that the number you hold is closer to 24, it is unlikely. For this reason, you should probably not get too adventurous with your overcalls.

Also, when your team is vulnerable, you should be even more cautious about overcalls and responses to overcalls because of the larger penalties if you fail. Be sure you have a long, strong suit, especially if you bid at the two level or higher. A good rule to follow is that your cards should be strong enough that you could win enough tricks on your own—without any help from your partner—to be within two tricks of your bid.

If your opponents are vulnerable, it can be acceptable to make overcalls with weaker hands. The longer your suit is, the fewer points are needed to make an overcall or to respond to one, especially if you and your partner also have great suit fit. So, under these circumstances you should compete aggressively for the contract. Penalties for not making your contract are relatively small, and it's better than losing the rubber, since your opponents will get a 700-point bonus, plus the value of their game. This is probably the only time when it's okay to take such a big, but calculated, risk.

Here are some basic guidelines for overcalling. With only 5 to 9 points, don't overcall unless you have a really long suit of six or more. If you have 10 to 12 points, and a good 5-plus suit, don't venture beyond the one level. With 12 to 15 points, a non-jump overcall would be acceptable (e.g., an overcall of two diamonds after an opponent's bid of one heart). A one no-trump overcall would be okay with 15 to 18 points, a balanced hand, and a few high-value face cards (e.g., aces and/or kings) in the suit the opponents are bidding. A takeout double should only be used with 12 or more points, shortness in the opponent's bidding suit, and at least three cards in all other suits, preferably high-value face cards. As explained earlier, this takeout double asks your partner to bid at the next possible level in their longest suit.

What's Next?

Now that you have read through and hopefully understood the information presented in the first three chapters of this book, including the guidelines for making opening bids and responding to opening bids, you know the basics of playing Bridge. So, I recommend that you now set this book aside and go play some Bridge, either with friends or using some type of computer game software or app. Getting multiple Bridge rubbers under your belt at this point will benefit you greatly. The remaining chapters of this book will provide you with valuable information you can use to enhance your playing of the game; it is not essential information for getting you started playing Bridge.

Chapter 4:
Bidding

The primary goal of any team during a Bridge auction should be to reach a contract that will score at least 100 points and win a game. You never want to miss out on an opportunity to get a game score on the scoresheet by being overly cautious and failing to set the commitment of your team high enough. However, many times it will not even be possible to reach a game-level contract with the cards you have, so your team will frequently have to settle for a partial-game score.

It is important that you do not see this as a failure. If you don't have the cards, you don't have the cards. It would, however, be a failure if you end the auction with a game-level contract when the cards you hold do not support such a gamble and you end up giving your opponents a large defensive point score. Of course, if you already have a partial score toward winning a game on the scoresheet, bidding to any level higher than what you need to win that game would probably also not be worth the risk. With more experience and good communication between you and your partner, you will learn when and when not to try for a game-level contract.

In any event, another thing you should always keep in mind when choosing a contract, no matter the level, is the different trick values for major suits, minor suits, and no-trump. That is also important information when assessing the risk involved in various contract options.

To review, the trick scores for each suit are the following:

Minor-suit contracts (♦ and ♣) award 20 points per trick past book. To win a game, you would need to bid up to at least a level of 5♣ or 5♦. Thus, you would need to win eleven of the thirteen possible tricks.

Major-suit contracts (♥ and ♠) award 30 points per trick past book. To win a game, you would need to bid up to at least a level of 4♥ or 4♠. Thus, you would need to win ten of the thirteen possible tricks.

In a no trump contract, you are awarded 40 points for the first trick past book and 30 points for all subsequent tricks. You will win a game if you bid up to at least (and successfully complete) 3NT, or win nine total tricks.

When you can get your contract to a game-winning level, and it makes sense to do so, it is always preferable to reach a four-trick contract in a major suit (e.g., four spades or four hearts).

Each trick won above book is worth 30 points, and you only need to win four above book (ten total) to win a game. This type of contract has the best reward-to-risk ratio. When that is not possible, a three no-trump contract is the next most preferable option, in part because you only need to win nine tricks to win a game. The lowest-priority option would be a five-trick contract in a minor suit, because each trick is worth only 20 points, and to win a game you will need to win eleven of the thirteen total tricks.

Bidding to Game in a Major Suit

Assume these are your cards. Do you make an opening bid? If so, what do you bid?

♠ A84 ♥ AJ7543 ♣ A3 ♦ K8

Because you have at least 13 points total, at least 10 FCPs, and six hearts, the correct opening bid would be one heart. Let's assume that the opponent to your left does not overcall your bid. Now it is up to your partner to respond to your bid. Assume that this is their hand:

♠ J7 ♥K862 ♣ K72 ♦ Q952

Given that they have at least 6 total points, 9 FCPs, and four hearts, their cards clearly meet the minimum conditions for responding, and they should most certainly respond. The correct response would be to raise your opening bid to two hearts.

Given that response, what conclusions can you draw? Well, you now know that they hold at least 6 FCPs. And since you know that you actually have 16 FCPs, 4 distribution points (six hearts, two doubletons), and a total of 20 points, that brings the total held by your team to at least 26 points. You can also now conclude that your six hearts combined with their four gives your team at least ten hearts.

Let's assume the opponent to your right also passes. What do you do next? With the information you now have, the correct bid at this point would be four hearts. That is because the collective experience of Bridge players in the past has shown that in most cases by far, a combined total of at least 26 points, with at least eight cards in the trump suit, will be enough to complete a four-trick contract in a major suit. And now, with your response of four hearts, your partner also gains more information regarding the characteristics of your cards—as do your opponents. More specifically, they now know that you and your partner hold cards worth at least 26 points, and that you hold at least eight hearts.

Of course, if your partner is the one making an opening bid of one heart or one spade, thus making you the responder, this example should allow you to also take the other perspective and to understand your role as your team tries to get to a game-winning contract.

Moreover, this example represents the best-case scenario when everything falls into place. Unfortunately, that is often not the case in Bridge. To begin with, your opponents might have other ideas. If you find yourself in competitive bidding for the contract with one or both of your opponents, you should be more cautious. This likely means that the FCPs your team does not hold could be concentrated in the hand of the opponent who is bidding against you. We will discuss competitive bidding and overcall bidding tactics and risks in more detail in a later chapter.

And, no matter what your hand looks like, there is always a very good chance that your partner does not have the points to respond to you at all. When that happens, you need to not only be able to understand and accept what your partner is saying to you, but also be willing to be pragmatic and settle for the best you can do.

Sometimes, your cards will have unusual characteristics that confuse things and make it difficult for you to know how to bid, respond, or how to bid to game. Here are a few common situations you may encounter, even when you have enough points to open the bidding.

If you have six cards in a one major suit and five in another, and your FCPs are mostly in the five-card suit, make the bid in your longest major suit to communicate the strength of your hand to your partner. You can always switch to your other five-card major suit in the second round of bidding.

If you have a four-card major suit and a five-card major, open in the longer suit.

If you have two four-card majors, bid one heart. This does not deny the value of your four spades but allows your partner, should they have four spades but not four hearts, to continue describing their hand by bidding one spade. You can raise the bidding to the needed level at your next turn.

If you have five cards in each major suit, start the bidding with one heart. You may have a chance to bid spades later to show your second suit.

Bidding to Game in No-Trump

If you examine your cards and they are worth 16 to 18 points, with all of the points coming from face cards (with FCPs in at least three of the four suits), and there is a relatively balanced distribution of suits (e.g., 4-3-3-3 or 4-4-3-2), you have met the basic conditions for an opening bid of one no-trump. It important here to take a moment to make sure that you understand what exactly such a bid is saying. You are proposing to win at least seven tricks, with no suit as a trump suit, based only on the face value of the cards you are holding (at this point). Furthermore, because of some unique risks in any no-trump contract, you should never open with a bid of one no-trump if you fail to meet any of these requirements. You would be better off opening at the one level with some suit as a trump suit.

If you do choose to open the bidding at one no-trump, what are the appropriate responses for your partner?

The first thing to keep in mind is that these guidelines only apply when the one no-trump bid is truly an opening bid. If you or your partner open the bidding at the one level in some suit, then a follow-up bid of one no-trump is not an opening bid, and it does not have the same meaning. It would therefore require a different response.

Moreover, if you or your partner choose to open with a bid of one no-trump, the respondent should not count points for doubletons, singletons, or voids toward the total of points in their hand, when deciding how to respond. It's impossible to **ruff** anything in a no-trump contract, so your short suits don't have any real trick-taking value.

With these thoughts in mind, here are some possible responses to a one no-trump opening bid.

If you have less than 8 points and no five-card major suit, you should pass.

With a five-card major suit—regardless of the strength of your cards—you should ALWAYS respond in one of two ways. This convention is called the **Jacoby transfer**.

If you have five or more hearts, your response should be two diamonds. This tells your partner that your longest suit is hearts.

If you have five or more spades, your response should be two hearts, which tells your partner that your longest suit is spades.

Your partner will then respond by bidding either two hearts or two spades, respectively. And, in some variations of this convention, it may be customary for your partner to verbally say the word "transfer" before responding to your one no-trump Jacoby transfer response.

With 8 or more points and a four-card major suit, the appropriate response is the **Stayman** convention. Your response to your partner's one no-trump opening bid should be two clubs, which is instructing your partner to respond at the two level in their four-card major suit if they have one.

With no four-card major suit, your partner should bid two diamonds, which means, "I do not have a four-card major." Now you have to decide what to do. And at this point, the strength of your hand should guide you. But remember, in this situation, only FCPs matter. Distribution points are not relevant and should not be used in assessing the strength of your cards.

If you have fewer than 8 FCPs, you should pass, thus leaving the contract at the two level.

If you have 8 to 9 FCPs and at least four cards in the major suit bid by your partner, the correct response would be to raise to the three level in that major suit (e.g., three hearts).

However, with 8 to 9 FCPs, and no fit in the major suit of your partner, the correct response is two no-trump.

With 8 or more FCPs, and a long minor suit (at least six), your response should be at the three level in your minor suit.

If you have 10 or more FCPs, and four more of the major suit, jump to the four level and game (e.g., four hearts).

However, with 10 or more FCPs, and no fit in the major of your partner, you should go to a game level and bid three no-trump.

Other examples:

Your cards: ♠AK7 ♥KJ6 ♦Q85 ♣AQ84

You have 19 FCPs in your hand, a balanced distribution of suits, and FCPs in at least three of your suits. You can open at one no-trump.

Your cards: ♠76 ♥AQ6 ♦AKQJ ♣8743

It is never a good idea to open one no-trump with FCPs in only two suits, even though you have many face cards in those two suits.

If you can open the bidding with one no-trump and eventually get to game of three no-trump, this is obviously a good situation to be in. In addition to needing to win only nine tricks to complete the contract, it is also a game-winning contract. Additionally, with the higher point totals required for opening and responding, and the source of those points being all face cards, the outcome of playing the hand will be a lot more predictable and hence will have lower risk.

Bidding to Game in a Minor Suit

Getting to a game-winning level contract in a minor suit (give tricks above book) is much riskier than game level in a major suit, or even no-trump, because you need to win eleven of the thirteen tricks. Only under a very special set of circumstances is going to a level of five in a minor suit worth the risk. So, when you have exhausted all other options, and you are left in a minor suit, you should be quite willing to settle for a contract at the three (partial-game) level.

Nevertheless, if you have at least 13 points and at least four cards in a minor suit, you can open at the one level of that suit.

If the opening bid is one club or one diamond, the first priority of the responder should always be to try to find a major-suit fit with their partner. This is preferable because, as stated earlier, fewer tricks need to be won in order to get a game-winning score. So, if you have at least 6 FCPs, and at least one four-card major suit, your first response should be a bid at the one level in that suit.

From the perspective of the opening bidder, if your partner has answered one club to your opening, and you at least have four cards in that major suit, and you have 12 to 15 points, you should raise the bid to two hearts. If you have 16 to 18 points, jump the bid up to three hearts, or four hearts with 19 or more support points. The same applies to the one-spade response when you have four-card support in that suit.

But, if your partner responds to your one-club bid with one heart or one spade, and you have 12 to 15 points in your hand and at least six clubs, rebid clubs at level two. If you have 16 to 18 points, jump the bid up to level three. The same is true if your opening bid is one diamond.

Here are some other points you should focus on after opening at one of a minor suit.

If your partner passes in response to your one-club bid, they are saying that they have no major suits with at least four cards. Stop there.

If your partner responds to your one-club bid with one diamond, then ask for information regarding their best major suit by bidding one heart. If spades is their longest major suit, they can then respond with one spade, or go to two hearts if that is longer, which is a bit riskier.

If your partner responds to your one-club bid with one heart, and you do not have at least four hearts, respond with one spade.

More examples:

Let's say your partner has opened with one diamond. What will be your best bid if you have the following hands?

Your cards: ♠ 987 ♥ K765 ♦ AQJ76 ♣ 8

You have a great suit fit with your partner's one-diamond opening and 10 FCPs. Your response should be one heart. If you raise diamonds first, your partner will not know about your four-card major: Remember, your priority should always be to try to find a major suit fit. If your partner then raises your hearts bid, your hand increases in value, and it would not be outrageous to invite your partner to a game level by bidding three hearts, or even jumping to four hearts.

Your cards: ♠ A98 ♥ K765 ♦ AJ107 ♣97

Even with 12 FCPs, you will still respond with one heart. However, if your partner raises your bid to two hearts, go straight for a game at four hearts. If your partner bids one spade, jump bid to game (i.e., four spades). However, if your partner responds to your one-heart bid with one no-trump, denying four-card support for your major suit, you should then respond with a bid of three no-trump.

Your cards: ♠ AJ9 ♥ AKJ765 ♦ Q4 ♣ K6

Under these circumstances, you should still bid one heart, but with a big smile inside. You have 22 points total, and your partner opened at one club/diamond, which promises at least 13 points. So, between the two of you, you have at least 35 total points, and at least 28 FCPs. In this situation, you will surely make a game-winning contract. You may even be able to reach at least a small-slam level. For example, if your partner rebids in diamonds, showing at least six of them, you should seriously consider a contract for a small slam in diamonds.

Your cards: ♠ 986 ♥ K75 ♦ AQJ74 ♣ 87

You should bid three diamonds. This is a jump bid and will tell your partner that you have 10 to 12 FCPs, no four-card major suit, but at least four diamonds. Most likely, this situation will lead to a three no-trump contract, so you should not count distributional points when making a jump-shift in a minor suit.

Your cards: ♠ KJ10 ♥ AQ8 ♦QJ96 ♣985

You should bid two no-trump. This bid shows that you have a balanced distribution and enough FCPs to win the game. You are also saying that you do not have a four-card major.

Your cards: ♠ 987 ♥ 765 ♦ AQJ76 ♣ 86

Your bid should be two diamonds. This is your best option. You don't have a lot of high cards, but you have too much to consider passing. One no-trump is not a good option with such weakness in three suits. With so much strength in the diamond suit, it is likely that your partner, who obviously had enough FCPs to open, will able to win some tricks in the other suits.

More Aggressive Opening Bids

As mentioned in the previous chapter, there may be situations where it would be entirely appropriate to open the bidding at the two level (in any suit) or no-trump. This bid is not only descriptive of the strength of your cards, but also a highly aggressive bid meant to intimidate your opponents into abandoning the auction. You are in effect saying, "My cards are so strong, you proceed at your own peril."

For example:

Your cards: ♠AQ10976 ♥ AK7 ♦AK4 ♣78

With 23 points and at least 10 FCPs, you should open at the two level. Your longest suit is clearly spades, with two face cards in three different suits. The appropriate opening bid here would be two spades. That would tell your partner that you have particularly strong cards, and if they can offer you any help at all, they can jump directly to a four-spades contract. However, if your partner responds with two no-trump, they are telling you that they have very little support, so don't go any further.

More examples:

You open by bidding two clubs. This communicates very powerful cards, with 22 or more FCPs and balance. If unbalanced, the cards likely still have a lot of trick-taking power, usually from a suit that is both long and powerful.

With 21 to23 points and a balanced distribution, you can open the bidding at two no-trump.

With 24 to25 FCPs, balance, or a long minor suit of at least seven cards headed by the AKQ, an opening of three no-trump would be appropriate.

Another form of aggressive (very risky) bidding is opening with especially weak cards or an unusual card distribution. For example, if your cards fall short of the 12 or 13 total points and/or 10 FCPs, under some circumstances you may still be able to open the bidding.

The Rule of 20

Count the number of cards in your two longest suits and add them together. Then add the number of FCPs. If the total is 20 or more, it may be acceptable to open the bidding process. However, players who use this approach need to understand that it is a high-risk move. The Rule of the 20 is a useful guideline but should not be followed blindly.

Example:

Your cards: ♠A9732 ♥AJ965 ♦J7 ♣ 7

Using the Rule of 20, you have 10 FCPs. Now, add to that the number of cards in your two longest suits, hearts and spades. The result is 20. This is a very respectable opener, and if your partner has a lot of support for one of your suits, you have a chance to take a lot of tricks.

Your cards: ♠107642 ♥97543 ♦AQ ♣A

The two long suits are very weak and the face-card strength is in the short minor suits. Yet, this hand also meets the requirements for the Rule of 20 because there are 10 FCPs and 10 cards in the hearts and spades suits. It would be irresponsible to open with these cards. However, if the ace and queen of diamonds were in the spade suit and the ace of clubs in the heart suit, you could open with one spade.

Another situation you might face is weak cards on points, but a seven-plus-card suit. Under certain conditions, opening at the three level, or even the four level in a major suit, might be appropriate. With an eight-plus-card minor suit, an opening bid of four of that minor, or even five of that minor, might be appropriate. With an eight-card-long major suit, of course, you would not need to go beyond the four level.

Again, these are very risky moves, and may only be worth it if you are on the verge of losing a rubber anyhow, and/or when you have a lot more experience as a Bridge player.

Chapter 5:
Competitive Bidding

When the cards dealt to you and your partner are strong enough that your team can bid your way into a game-winning contract with little or no interference from your opponents, you are very fortunate. However, such situations are unusual. More commonly, you will become involved in competitive bidding for the contract, either because your opponents opened the bidding before you had a chance to speak, or because they overcalled your opening bid. In such situations, your impulse to be aggressive in the bidding, as you try to reach a game-winning contract, should be tempered by caution.

Responding to an Opponent's Opening

When your opponents are the first to bid, the risk of your team losing the auction is immediately increased. Deciding what to do next can often be difficult, especially if you also have strong cards. One obvious option is to simply accept your fate and pass. Of course, the result of that choice may be that you have to watch helplessly as your opponents bid up to, and complete, a game-winning contract. However, another option is for your team to also enter the auction with the hope that you can wrest the contract away from your opponents and at least complete a partial game.

Assuming that entering the auction is the option you choose, there are several tactics you can utilize to proceed while simultaneously minimizing the risk. One such approach is to overcall, but with a pre-established agreement between you and your partner regarding the circumstances under which overcalls will be made and at what level they will be abandoned. This **limited overcalling** concedes nothing to your opponents because it still challenges them directly for the contract. But it also keeps the risk at a manageable level.

Overcalling

If you bid one spade in response to an opponent's bid of one heart, your bid is an overcall. To overcall at the one level, you should have at least 8 FCPs, and a long suit (five or more). If you have at least 12 FCPs and at least two aces or kings, along with a few lower value cards in each suit, an overcall at the two level would be appropriate. With 13 or more FCPs, and a long suit of six or more, you should definitely consider overcalling.

Moreover, with your overcall, you are not just proposing a contract as part of the auction. You are also communicating to your partner that you have decent cards and a long suit. Thus, "We should consider competing for this contract." Of course, you should also keep in mind that at least one your opponents clearly has some card strength because they opened the bidding. You shouldn't get too overconfident or reckless. This is why "limits" on overcalling make sense.

When the opponents open at one club or one diamond, you do have lots of **bidding space** left on the one level with two major suit options. Therefore, overcalling at one level is relatively safe because, even if you get the contract, you only need to win seven tricks. And, if you are unsuccessful at completing the contract, the penalty points scored by your opponents would be minimal.

For example:

Your cards: ♠ AKJ75 ♥ 75 ♦ 9753 ♣ 87

Assume the opponent to your right opens with one heart. You evaluate your cards and decide that you certainly should get into the auction, so you overcall at one spade. Your opponents must now decide what to do next. They would need to bid at least one no-trump in order to remain in the auction. The only other option is to stay with hearts as the trump suit, and raise the bidding up to two hearts. They may determine that the risk of choosing either option is too high, and thus decide not to go any further. The result is that, because you chose to compete for the contract rather than just give up, you win the auction and pull the contract away from your opponents.

Similarly, if your opponent's opening bid is one diamond, it would be entirely reasonable to overcall at one heart with these cards.

Your cards: ♠ Q64 ♥ AKJ54 ♦ 109 ♣ 743

However, if the opening bid on your right is one spade, it would be dangerous to overcall at the two level based on a five-card heart suit, with only 10 FCPs, and 11 points total. That is too far away from the minimum required for a two-level overcall. And, if you are also vulnerable, it would be suicidal.

An appropriate two-level overcall situation, when not vulnerable, would look like this:

Your cards: ♠ 432 ♥ AKJ1063 ♦ Q4 ♣ 102

An acceptable two-level overcall situation, when vulnerable, would look more like this:

Your cards: ♠ 764 ♥ AKJ1098 ♦ K9 ♣ K10

These cards are worth 18 points, which is the bare minimum for a two-level overcall when vulnerable.

Of course, not overcalling when it would be appropriate also has a downside: a missed opportunity. For example, if you have a legitimate one-level overcall situation but decide to pass, you may regret it later. The following situation is not uncommon:

Your cards: ♠ 98 ♥ QJ987 ♦ Q10 ♣ KJ63 as North.

And the auction proceeds as follows:

WEST	NORTHEAST		SOUTH
1♣	Pass	2♣	Pass
4♣	Pass	Pass	?

Your cards clearly support a one-heart overcall, but you choose to pass. Your partner (South) may have had some hearts to support you and perhaps even enough to make four Hearts. Unfortunately, your failure to communicate effectively with your partner by not overcalling with a one-heart bid means that you will now never know what could have been possible. And you clearly do not have the cards for an overcall at the four level. That would likely result in a disaster. Your decision not to act earlier has now left you with no choice but to pass.

Overcalling can also sometimes be useful for communicating to your partner what suit to lead with when your opponents win the auction, or to at least let your partner know your longest suit.

One of the most important benefits of overcalling in Bridge is that it can often interfere with the bidding of your opponents and force them out of their comfort zone. For example, because of your overcall, you may be able to get your opponents to bid up to three hearts instead of just two hearts, thus making it less likely that they will be successful in completing their contract. In other circumstances, you may be able to push them into a different trump suit than the one they prefer, or even push them into a no-trump contract when the strength of their cards really does not support such a venture.

Finally, overcalling in no-trump typically has a special meaning. An overcall of one no-trump communicates 15 to 18 FCPs, and an overcall of two no- trump promises at least five cards in each of the two lowest unbid suits.

Other Competitive Bidding Tactics

As alternatives to overcalling, Bridge players have devised a variety of other less risky ways of testing the waters for a possible contract during a competitive auction. These tactics minimize risk by increasing the information communicated between partners, and include takeout doubles, **cue-bids**, and **balancing** the bidding. When deciding how and when to use any of these tactics, the strength of your cards, the level reached in the bidding, your position at the table relative to the opponent who opened the bidding, the suit mentioned in the opening bid, your team's vulnerability, and your team's position in the rubber should always be taken into consideration.

The Takeout Double

Assume that one of your opponents has opened the bidding at one heart and you are seated just to the left of that opponent. As discussed in a previous chapter, under certain circumstances you could say "double" when it is your turn to speak. This would immediately be recognized by all of the players as a takeout double because you have said it in a situation where a issuing a penalty-double challenge would be inappropriate. Therefore, it is reasonable to assume that it must have some other meaning. In other words, you are not saying to the other team, "I don't think you can complete such a contract." Instead, you are telling your partner that you have cards worth 11 or more points, and at least three-card support for the three suits not mentioned by your opponents. Moreover, you are insisting that your partner bid at the next possible level in their strongest (or longest) unbid suit. Passing is not an option.

Why is your partner not allowed to pass? To do so would convert your takeout double into a penalty double, and that has two immediate consequences. First, as with any penalty double, it doubles the amount of points your opponents can earn by winning and completing a contract. In a major suit, this could cost you a game. Secondly, it reduces the risk of your opponents. As a result of the double, they may be able to score enough points to win, or get closer to winning a game, without actually having to bid up to that level. In response to a takeout double, the partner should always respond by bidding in some way.

Like an overcall, a takeout double also gets your team into the auction and allows you to begin to explore the possibility of a contract for your team. However, it is a safer option than an overcall, because it does not risk leaving your team in some trump-suit contract that you may not be able to complete. This is especially true when an overcall might leave you with an undesirable contract at the two level or higher.

Furthermore, a takeout double does not have to be issued immediately after an opening bid. Once the bidding has passed to them, the third player to bid after an opening can also issue a takeout double. However, the circumstances under which this is done, and the reasons for doing it, are very different. For example, if West issues an opening bid of one club, your partner passes, and then East bids one heart, you could then issue a takeout double. In this situation, the takeout double communicates to your partner that you hold cards worth 11 or more points, with three-card support only for diamonds and spades. It is also requesting that your partner respond with a bid in either diamonds or spades, whichever is strongest, with passing not being an option.

As with overcalls, partners will often have some type of pre-established agreement on when and how high to go with takeout doubles. For example, you might agree to play takeout doubles through the three level, and penalty doubles only at the four level or higher.

Responding to Takeout Doubles

If your partner issues a takeout double of the opening bid and the next player passes, the spotlight is now on you. As you examine your cards, you should be assessing how much support you can give to your partner in each of the unmentioned suits. Furthermore, any face cards from the opening opponent's suit should be discounted, or at least devalued, except for the ace. Remember, when your partner issues a takeout double, they are telling you (in part) that they are short in the opener's suit.

Even if you have 0 to 8 FCPs, do not pass. Bid your strongest unbid suit at the minimum level. For example, if the opening bid was one club and your best unbid suit is hearts, then bid one heart.

If you have 9 to 11 FCPs and a suit with four or more cards, then you should make a jump-shift bid in that suit. For example, if the opening bid was one diamond and spades is your best suit, then your response to the takeout double should be two spades.

If you have 13 or more points and an unbid suit with five or more cards, a double jump-shift in that suit might be an appropriate response to your partner's takeout. For example, if the opening was one spade and clubs is your best suit, then your response should be three clubs. Under these circumstances, you are also telling your partner that being any more aggressive in competing for the contract would not be warranted.

If you have at least 14 to 17 FCPs and a long and strong unbid suit (e.g., ♠ KQJ985 or ♥KJ10976), a jump-bid to a game-level contract in the strong suit would be the appropriate response. You are likely to win the contract under these circumstances, and so now the greater risk has shifted back to your opponents.

Under certain conditions, it might also be appropriate to respond to a takeout double with a response of one no trump (e.g., you have 8 to 11 FCPs, balance, and a **stopper** [e.g., A or K] in the opponent's opening suit).

With 11 to 13 points, balance, and a stopper in the opponent's suit, a jump- shift into no-trump would be acceptable (e.g., responding to a takeout double of one club with two no-trump).

With 14 to 17 points, balance, and a trump stopper, jump to a three no-trump sign-off bid.

Suppose your partner responds to a bid of one club with a takeout double and the next player passes, what is your response if you hold the following hands?

Your cards: ♠ KQ7 ♥ 62 ♦ J1096 ♣ 8642

You should bid one diamond. You have only 1 FCP in that suit, but it would not be a good idea to make a one-spade bid based only on three cards in that suit.

Remember, your partner could have as few as three spades and still have a hand that qualifies for issuing a takeout double.

Your cards: ♠ 82 ♥ KQJ5 ♦ QJ65 ♣ 763

Your hand is too good for a simple one-heart response. With 0 to 8 FCPs, and any four weak Hearts, you could have responded with one heart. Your cards are a lot better than that. You need to let your partner know when your hand is well above the minimum. So, a jump-bid at two hearts would be appropriate.

The Cue-bid

A cue-bid is bidding in the same suit as your opponent's previous bid, whether it was an opening bid or an overcall. For example, if you bid two hearts in response to an opponent's opening of one heart, you have issued a cue-bid. Like a Jacoby transfer or a takeout double, it is "artificial" because it is not intended to express a preference for a contract in a particular suit. Instead, its primary purpose is to request information from your partner or to communicate information to your partner. For that reason, like a takeout double, it should always be responded to in some way.

There are many different types of cue-bids used in different situations. One of the most commonly used is the **Michaels cue-bid**. If a player opens the bidding at the one level of a suit and the next player (an opponent) bids two of the same suit (e.g., two clubs in response to one club), they have made a Michaels cue-bid. Basically, it communicates at least 8 points and at least five cards in two different suits. It also requests that the player's partner respond by bidding at the next possible level in their best suit. It is especially useful in situations where the players have strong cards, but they are not strong enough for a takeout double.

Depending on the opening suit, the cue-bid can also communicate even more specific information. A cue-bid of the opponent's opening in a minor suit communicates strength in both major suits. However, a cue-bid of the opponent's major suit communicates strength in the other major suit and either of the two minor suits. For example, if one of your opponents opened with a bid of one club and your partner overcalled with one spade, a response of two clubs (the same suit of your opponent's opening bid) would communicate that you have at least 10 support points and support in spades.

Of course, you could have responded with two spades. But think about the situation you are facing. One of your opponents has already opened in clubs, so you can conclude that they have cards worth at least 13 points. Then your partner overcalled, which suggests a possible trump suit match in spades and some decent FCPs. However, at this point you don't know how many FCPs. A response of two spades would be too risky in this situation, because if your partner's FCPs are on the low side, you could end up in a spades contract doomed to failure. So, the cue-bid of two clubs gives you a safer way to let your partner know that you at least like the idea of a spades contract, while leaving it up to them to have the final say on feasibility.

There is also one situation when you can use a cue-bid in response to a takeout double: when your partner doubles the opponent's opening of a minor suit and you have strength in both major suits.

For example:

Your cards: ♠ KQJ3 ♥ QJ62 ♦ Q9 ♣ 763

These cards are good enough to make a jump-bid to tell your partner that a game-level contract is possible. But which major should you choose? You could end up with only seven trumps instead of eight if you guess incorrectly. So, a bid of two clubs would be a safer approach. Your partner will recognize this as a cue-bid, and if they have one major suit of at least four cards, they can then respond to you in that suit. If they have five cards in each suit, then two hearts would be the appropriate response. You can then raise to three hearts to show that your cue-bid was indeed intended as an invitation to game.

Now your partner can make the final decision about whether or not to go to a game level, and you have provided your partner with valuable information that should help them in making that decision. However, be careful about cue-bidding in response to a takeout double without sufficient card strength to possibly lead you to game level. If your cards fall short, simply bid the higher-ranking suit at the one level, even if they are the same length.

Balancing the Bidding

Often, it will very quickly become obvious to you and/or your partner if your cards are probably not strong enough win the auction and establish the contract. There is no need for despair. For this particular auction, you can just shift your posture from a competitive (or offensive) one to a largely defensive one. In other words, you can change from a strategy of working to win the auction, to a strategy of interference, obstruction, and disruption.

One such disruption tactic you can use is called **balancing** the bidding. Balancing is normally done when your cards are not strong enough for direct action, and when your opponents' bidding has demonstrated weakness or minimal strength. The primary purpose of this tactic is to force your opponents to raise the stakes, so when they fail, they will be penalized more. Balancing is also typically done by the player whose pass would end the auction and leave their opponents with a contract at the one or two level. This position at the table is often referred to as the balancing position or seat, and balancing can be achieved either by a strategic overcall, a Michaels cue-bid, or by issuing a takeout double.

Suppose the bidding goes in the following way:

WEST	NORTH	EAST	SOUTH
1 ♥	Pass	Pass	?

Notice what East did in response to West's opening bid. This pass tells you that East did not have even the minimum amount of card points to respond. In fact, neither of your opponents seem to have particularly strong cards. If West had more than minimum opening points, they might have made a more aggressive bid. More likely, they have only 12 or 13 FCPs, and the responding partner apparently has less than has 6, which at best Is around 18 FCPs in total for their team.

Your cards: ♠ Q987 ♥ 32 ♦KQ65 ♣ K109

Assume you are South and it's your turn to bid. Your opponents seem to be willing to play for a contract of one heart.

You definitely should not let them win the auction so easily by just passing. Since, you know that you have 10 FCPs, and your opponents' cards are weak, your partner will probably have around 10 to -12 points as well. In other words, it's reasonable to assume that the FCPs are fairly evenly distributed between the two teams. The approximately 20 to 22 points held by your team certainly should be enough points to make things difficult for your opponents. So, what can you do?

You clearly don't have enough strength to overcall at one spade, but you could do a takeout double, even if you only have 10 FCPs. Then, as a result, West must make a difficult decision. "Do we stay at the one level and risk losing the contract to the other team?" Remember, in response to your obvious takeout double, your partner must respond (West knows that also), and so, if West now passes, your partner can still bid one spade. The only other option is to continue to compete for the contract by making the risky move of responding with two hearts, which the strength of their cards may not support. In other words, your takeout double has had the intended effect of making things more difficult for your opponents, and West in particular.

Another situation could be as follows:

Your cards: ♠ Q3 ♥ QJ32 ♦KJ852 ♣ 96

And suppose the bidding goes in the following way:

WEST	NORTH	EAST	SOUTH
1♣	Pass	2♣	2♦

In this situation, as the last bidder before the contract is awarded to your opponents at two clubs, your response of two diamonds forces your opponents to face the choice of either switching their proposed contract to a different major suit (away from their suit strength) so they can remain at the two level, or risk going to the three level in clubs, which their cards likely do not support. The only other option is to abandon the auction completely. This type of interference with the opponents' bidding is precisely the purpose of the balancing-the-bidding tactic.

Under certain circumstances, however, balancing the bidding would not be appropriate—even when the opponent stops at a low level. For example, you would pass if you held these cards.

Your cards: ♠A7 ♥QJ98 ♦K752 ♣863

Assume that your opponents have opened in your best suit. That, combined with your holding in hearts, makes it clear your partner likely has very few hearts. Furthermore, they took no action, indicating they also have few FCPs. If your team is vulnerable, you should be even more very leery of "balancing" under these circumstances.

Preemptive Bidding

There is another bidding tactic that is used only by very experienced Bridge players, and rightly so. It is called a **preemptive bid**, and it is extremely risky. Specifically, you risk getting stuck in a very high-level contract that you have little or no hope of completing and giving your opponents a lot of penalty points. However, under certain conditions, such a gamble may be worth the risk. The assumption you would be making is that, even if your bid is doubled, the penalty will still be smaller than the value of the opponents' bid and made doubled contract.

Sometimes, a player does not have enough FCPs to issue a standard opening bid, but does hold a long suit (e.g., six to nine cards), with most of the FCPs in that long Suit. If the player then offers an opening bid at some level higher than the one level, this is preemptive bidding. A general rule to follow is that you can preempt at the two level with a six-card long suit, preempt at the three level with a seven-card long suit, and preempt at the four level with an eight-card long suit.

When you open the bidding, or even overcall, by preempting, you accomplish at least two things.

First, you tell your partner about your long suit, and are essentially saying, "I have six (or seven to eight) cards in this suit. If you have enough points for an opening bid, then pass, and we can play out a contract in my long suit." It is a big gamble and may even be described as an act of desperation, but it can be an effective tactic sometimes.

At the same time, you are taking bidding space away from your opponents by preventing (or "preempting") them from making normal bids because they can no longer open at any level below your opening bid. So, your preemption is also a defensive tactic that interferes with the bidding plans of your opponents. With little or no bidding space left, the risk to your opponents of bidding anything at all has increased substantially. If they do bid at the level of your preemption or above it, more often than not they will guess wrong and you will score a lot of penalty points. But if you are lucky, and your partner does happen to have enough points to support your gamble, the reward could be a quick game-level contract that leaves your opponents stunned. Consequently, preemptive bidding, and knowing how to handle a preemptive bid, is probably best left for the most experienced players.

For example:

Your cards: ♠7 ♥KQJ98732 ♦863 ♣6

Your hand has a lot of strength to play hearts as the trump suit because you can be sure of seven tricks. The appropriate action is to open with a preemptive bid. This immediately informs your partner that your cards are weak and only useful if the contract is played in your long suit. If you are not vulnerable, your preemptive bid should be at the four level. However, if you are vulnerable, you should preempt only at the three level.

With the cards shown above, and you being not vulnerable, you would open or overcall at four hearts. If your partner then passes, that means that they do have the support you hoped for (at least three tricks), and so you can also pass on your next turn and accept the game-level contract. Even if you don't succeed, you consider it worth the risk because you prevent your opponents from winning the auction. Furthermore, you won't give up a lot of penalty points, with only three undertricks at most, even if you are doubled.

If you are vulnerable, you would open or overcall with three hearts, and if your opponent passes, then don't bid again. Your hand is still limited in strength and going any further is clearly not worth the risk.

When It seems likely that your opponents are headed for a game-level contract, there are four possible situations you might face.

If neither side is vulnerable, your opponents are likely to score 400 or 420 points from a doubled-game contract. However, your preemptive bid at the four level, when doubled, and if defeated by no more than two tricks, will cost you 300 penalty points at most.

If your team is not vulnerable but your opponents are, they would score 600 or 620 points from a doubled-game-level contract, while your preemptive bid at the four level, when doubled, and if defeated by no more than three tricks, will cost you 500 penalty points at most.

If your team is vulnerable and your opponents are not, they will score 400 or 420 points from a doubled-game contract, but your doubled bid at the three level, if defeated by no more than one trick, will cost you 200 penalty points at most.

When both sides are vulnerable, your opponents are likely to score 600 or 620 points at a doubled-game level, but your doubled bid at the three level, when defeated by no more than two tricks, will cost 500 penalty points at most.

In summary, when your opponents are likely to bid and make game, it may be advantageous to make a calculated risk and preempt. Specifically, you should be willing to: risk going down three tricks when your team is not vulnerable, but your opponents are vulnerable; risk going down two tricks when vulnerability is equal; and risk going down one trick when your team is vulnerable, but your opponents are not vulnerable.

A partner in cooperation with each other can also preempt their opponents. For example, after your partner opens with one club and your opponent in the fourth seat issues a takeout double, the following hand is suitable for a jump-raise to five clubs, taking away any hope your opponents might have had about finding a major suit fit for a game, as the takeout double was encouraging.

♠ 62 ♥ 8 ♦ QJ86 ♣ Q109432

Preemption can also be done as an overcall, and the requirements are basically the same as for a preemptive opening. However, they are normally relaxed for the third seat, when the first opponent and your partner have previously passed, and the opponent to your immediate right then opens. Your preemption can make it difficult for their partner to respond, and thus effectively interfere with their plans.

In summary, there are a variety of more (or less) risky things you can do to effectively compete with your opponents during the auction phase of a Bridge hand. Bridge is, after all, a competitive game. Finding the appropriate balance between a vigorous offense and a sensible and strategic defense is an essential part of the game.

⍰

Chapter 6:
Playing the Hand: Trump Contracts

O nce the auction has been completed and the contract awarded, the Bridge hand must be played out so that the success or failure of the contract can be determined. While this gameplay phase of the hand is somewhat less complicated than the auction phase, it can nevertheless be much more interesting. As is the case during the auction, the more information the player has available, the greater the chances of success and the lower the risk of failure. There are also many important skills, strategies, and techniques that can be learned in order to play a Bridge hand well, regardless if you are the declarer or the defenders.

Getting Started

Assume that your team has won the auction and, because you opened the bidding in the eventual trump suit, you are now the declarer. It has become your responsibility to play both your cards and the cards in the dummy hand, and try to win enough tricks to complete your contract. While sometimes predictable, every playing out of a Bridge hand can also present you with unique challenges and unfortunate surprises. All of your careful efforts during the auction, to insure that your team has a contract you can complete, will be wasted if you don't take this gameplay phase of the Bridge hand seriously and thus mess it up. You do not want to let down your partner in this way.

First and foremost, you should take your time. No one will be timing you to see how quickly you get the cards played out. Rushing through the gameplay can result in errors that create major problems. When the lead card is played, and before you play a card from the dummy hand, look at that card carefully and think about what it is telling you. Review in your mind any bidding by your opponents, and think about what face cards they might be holding, what length they might have in suits that they bid, or short suits they may hold. Then, when the dummy cards are revealed, take some time to look them over carefully, evaluate how your cards and the dummy cards fit together. At this point, you should at least be able to make an assessment about your earlier assumptions regarding various characteristics of your partner's cards (e.g., FCPs, trump suit length, short suits, etc.). Definitely, you should count how many trump cards your team holds, so you can know with certainty how many are held by your opponents. Then, determine and count the tricks you are certain to win, as well as your potential losing cards, in each suit. Finally, you need to decide when and in what order you will collect your winning tricks, how you might be able to establish additional winners, and what cards should be discarded when possible. In other words, develop an overall plan in your head for playing out the hand and completing the contract.

Examining the Lead

With you as the declarer, the opponent to your immediate left will be the one who leads the first card to begin the play, and you should immediately ask why this particular card was played. This is also why briefly reviewing the bidding in your head can be important. One common opponent lead is to start with a singleton that would immediately create a void in some suit for that player, thus allowing trump cards to be used as soon as possible. If the lead is a middle card in a suit that was not bid by either of your opponents, this is most likely the reason. Alternatively, if one of your opponents bid in a particular suit, their partner may lead with a low card in that suit, assuming that their partner has one or more face cards with which they can win that trick. Another approach may be to lead with a middle card in the suit bid by their partner, as a way of signaling to the partner that after they win the trick, they should lead back in the same suit, because that trick can then be won with another high face card. Of course, if their partner offered no bids, an opponent might choose to lead in a suit that your side did not bid, assuming that their partner may have high face cards in that suit with which they can then win that trick. In any event, what you can surmise about the characteristics of your opponents' cards based on their lead card, and even cards they might play later on, can be valuable information.

Counting Sure Tricks

As soon as the dummy cards are revealed, your team has one obvious advantage over your opponents. As the declarer, you can see all of the cards held by your team, while your opponents cannot. Furthermore, neither of your opponents can see all of the cards held by their team. With this informational advantage, one thing you can quickly and easily determine is how many **sure winners** you have in each suit.

Sure winners are tricks that you are guaranteed to win, if played one right after the other, without giving up the lead. For example, if you have an ace in the trump suit, it is a guaranteed win, because there is no other card playable during this hand that can beat it. Similarly, if you hold the ace, king, and queen of the trump suit, all three are guaranteed winners. Usually, an ace of any suit can also be counted as a sure win, unless an opponent just happens to have a void in that suit, enabling them to win that trick with a trump card. Unfortunately, that can happen, but it is rare. Typically, even an ace, king, and queen of a non-trump suit, either in your cards or in the dummy hand, or some combination of the two, may be counted on as sure winners as long as there is a relatively even distribution of the lower-ranked cards in that suit. And if you have length in your trump suit, either in your cards or in the dummy hand, at least some of those lower-value trump cards can also probably be counted on as sure winners—if the hand is played out correctly.

Once you have counted your sure winners and potential losers, in both the cards you hold and in the dummy hand, you will certainly have a better sense of how close you are to completing your contract. Only rarely will you have enough sure tricks to be guaranteed success, but if you played the auction well, you should always be pretty close.

The Play from the Dummy Hand

Now, you will need to decide which card from the dummy hand you will play on that first trick. As you decide, you should also be planning ahead about where you want to lead from on the next trick: the dummy hand or your hand. If on the next trick, for example, you know that you will want to lead from the cards in your hand, and you know that you can win that trick from your hand, then you should play the lowest card in that suit from the dummy hand. Obviously, it would not make sense to play a higher card on that trick, since you will be winning it in your hand anyhow, and you may be able to use that high card from the dummy hand to win another trick later on.

On the other hand, if you want to lead the next trick from the dummy hand, then you should play a high face card on the trick from the dummy hand, and then play a low card in that suit from the cards in your hand. During the remaining play out of the hand, there will be points at which it would be to your advantage to lead from the cards in your hand, or to your advantage to lead from the dummy hand. Thinking ahead as to which will be the best place to lead from at which point is a very important part of planning the playing out of the hand.

Establishing Winning Tricks

Clearly, your objective as the declarer is to win enough tricks to complete your contract, and there are many different ways of winning tricks. Two obvious ways are by using high face cards or trump cards.

While you may be tempted to begin by taking all of your guaranteed winning tricks in the non-trump suits or trump suit immediately, that is not always the best strategy. As mentioned earlier, it is unlikely that you will have enough sure tricks to achieve your contract. Fortunately, there are also a variety of other things you can do to create more sure winners, which will likely be necessary to get you over the top. Therefore, you should always keep a few sure face-card winners in case they are needed later to assist in that process. Also, if you lose the lead during the play, and are unable to get it back, especially in no-trump contracts, that can be a major headache. Having definite face-card winners or trump-card winners can immediately get the lead back for you.

There are other techniques you can also use to set up additional winning tricks by **promoting** cards, **establishing** voids and **ruffing**, establishing length winners, and/or **finessing**. Each of these techniques will now be discussed in more detail. They will also be discussed in the order in which you should probably be doing them, when possible, as you play out the hand.

Promoting Cards

The very first thing you should do in playing out the hand is establish the additional winning tricks you will need to complete your contract. One of the simplest ways of setting up additional winning tricks is by promoting cards. For example, let's assume that the cards you hold include the king, queen, and jack of a particular suit, but not the ace. Consequently, none of these face cards are guaranteed winners for you because each of them can be beaten by the ace. However, you can overcome this problem by encouraging (or forcing out) the play of the ace early on so it is no longer a threat. For example:

DUMMY
♠653

WEST
♠1092

EAST
♠A74

SOUTH
♠KQJ8

Assume that you are South, you have won the previous trick, and you now have the lead. You may now hope to win a few tricks in Spades. Since you do not have the ace of spades, however, that is a problem. Leading with the eight of spades would certainly result in the loss of the trick. West could play either the nine or the ten, and you have nothing in the dummy hand that could beat that, so then East, recognizing that West has already won the trick, would just play their seven or four. Meanwhile, the original problem has not been solved. The ace is still out there. Unfortunately, that will inevitably result in you losing another trick in Spades.

A better approach would be to lead with the king of spades (or the queen or jack), and this will undoubtedly resolve your ace problem. East can (and likely will) win the trick with the ace. Once that happens, your other two spade face cards have now been promoted into sure winners, because they are now the highest-ranking spades remaining. Once you get the lead back, you can then lead again in spades, either from your cards or the dummy hand, and likely win two additional tricks in spades. By promoting, you have added two more tricks to your tally of sure winners, whereas the other option (leading with the eight) would have guaranteed the loss of two tricks.

Establishing Voids

If the cards you are dealt contain a void in any suit, any leads by your opponents in that suit can obviously be trumped by you, allowing you to win the trick. When you win a trick in this manner, it is called a **ruff**. Moreover, using various tactics, you may also be able to strategically create voids, either in your hand or in the dummy hand, which can then allow you to win additional tricks by ruffing, or allow for the discarding of sure losing cards. Whenever it is possible to establish voids, this is also something you should do right away.

For example:

DUMMY
♥9863

WEST
♥AK54

EAST
♥QJ107

SOUTH
♥ 2

Assume spades is the trump suit and you have a few of them in your hand. West leads by playing the king of hearts to win a sure trick, since they also hold the ace. If there was no trump suit, West would then be able to also win the next trick with the ace, and then lead back to their partner, allowing East to then win two more tricks with the queen and jack. That would be four tricks won by the defenders. However, when West plays the king, that creates a void in your cards in hearts. So, when East then leads with the ace, you can ruff the trick by playing a spade, winning the trick for your side—much to the surprise of your opponents.

Similarly:

DUMMY
♠A10876

WEST   EAST
♠KQJ5   ♠9432

SOUTH
♠ -

Again, assume hearts is the trump suit and you still have a few of them in your hand. West leads the king of spades and now you can win the trick in two ways. Since you have a void in spades, you can play the six of spades from the dummy hand and then win the trick by playing a trump card from your hand. Alternatively, you can play the ace of spades from the dummy hand and discard a potential losing card (e.g., a low club or diamond), especially if that discard gets you to (or closer to) a void. Obviously, it would be unwise to play both the ace of spades and then a trump card since both could win a trick on their own.

Eliminating Losers

If you have potential losing cards in the dummy hand, it can also be a wise strategy to get the loss of those tricks completed as soon as possible and before you lead in the trump suit. **Losers** are tricks you know you will certainly lose. For example, if neither the declarer nor the dummy holds the ace in a suit, you know that you will likely lose at least one trick in that suit. Such obvious losers should also be dealt with as soon as possible. Moreover, there may be other sure losers that get set up during the course of playing out the Hand. So, you should also try to anticipate when and where that is likely to happen, and try to eliminate those potential losing cards by discarding them on other tricks whenever possible.

For example, assume the trump suit is diamonds, and hearts is a side suit. In the cards pictured below, you have two eventual losers in hearts. You do have the ace of hearts, effectively protecting one—but only one—of the low hearts in the dummy hand. As soon as your opponents lead a high heart card, thus forcing out your ace to promote their high heart face cards, your remaining two low heart cards become sure losers.

DUMMY

♥ 7 6 3

DECLARER

♥ A 8 4

If you are clever, however, you may be able to minimize this problem—if not prevent it completely. You may be able to eliminate one, or both, of these potential losing low heart cards by discarding them on other tricks where you cannot follow suit in the dummy hand—either on tricks you are willing to lose anyhow, or tricks you will be certain to win.

For example:

DUMMY

♥ 7 6 3 ♦ 3 ♠ A K 10 3

DECLARER

♥ A 8 4 ♦ A Q J ♠ J 8 4

112

You have the lead in your hand. Before leading with the ace of hearts, you could lead with the ace of diamonds and win that trick. At the same time, this would create a void in the dummy hand in diamonds. Then you could lead with either the queen or jack of diamonds from your hand, and wait to see what West does. If they play the king of diamonds in an attempt to win the trick, which they are very likely to do if they have it, then you can just play a low trump card and win that trick, while at the same time promoting your queen or jack of diamonds into a sure winner. However, if West does not play the king of diamonds, it is safe to conclude that East holds the king of diamonds. And because the dummy hand is now void in diamonds, you are not able to follow suit. So, you could just discard one of your two losing low heart cards on that trick and allow East to win the trick with the king. You have now eliminated one of your potential losing heart cards, and at the same time still promoted the jack of diamonds into a winner.

Getting Out the Trump

As discussed previously, if you lead with a card in a particular suit, and your opponent is unable to follow suit (because they have a void in that suit), that opponent can play a trump card on that suit and win the trick. Consequently, having a lot of trump cards in the hands of your opponents is a risky situation which you should eliminate as soon as possible. You can easily do this by making several leads in and winning tricks with trump cards, thus capturing the trump cards held by your opponents. As you do this, you should also keep track of (or **count**) the trump cards as they are played so you know when your opponents no longer hold any trumps.

One common approach to keeping track of trump cards is as follows: After the dummy hand has been revealed, you will know the exact number of trump cards held by your team and, more importantly, by your opponents. As trump cards are played by your opponents on future tricks, reduce the number of opponent trump cards in your mind until you reach zero.

Capturing all of the trump cards early on can also often promote remaining middle level face cards in other suits (e.g., queens, jacks, and tens) into definite winners, because it eliminates any possibility that they could be trumped. In fact, keeping track of which cards have been played in each of the suits would be a good skill to develop and use while playing Bridge.

For example, in the cards shown below, assume hearts is the trump suit. Obviously, you will lose two spade tricks. But, then you will be able to ruff the third round of spades because there will be a void in your hand. If you then lead with the six of diamonds, West has to play the ten of diamonds in order to follow suit. You then play the ace of diamonds from the dummy hand, East throws out a low diamond, and you win the trick.

DUMMY
♠752
♥1082
♦AKQ
♣A64

WEST
♠AKQJ4
♥96
♦10
♣109832

EAST
♠1096
♥754
♦J75432
♣J7

SOUTH
♠83
♥AKQJ3
♦986
♣KQ5

Do you see the problem? Unbeknownst to you, West has a singleton in diamonds. So, if you now lead with the king of diamonds, you are in for an unpleasant surprise. West trumps your ace, and all you can do is sit back and watch as one of your presumed sure winners is lost.

An alternative approach would be to eliminate the trump cards held by your opponents before you try to win with the cards you believe to be sure winners. In the cards illustrated above, your team holds eight trumps, which means that your opponents have five. Suppose that, before you play the diamond suit, your lead with the ace of hearts. West has to follow suit and plays the six, you play the two of hearts from the dummy hand, and then East plays the four. Now you know that your opponents hold only three more trumps. You now lead with the king of hearts, West plays the nine, you play the eight from the dummy hand, and East plays the five of hearts. Now you know that there is only one trump card left, and if you have been carefully keeping track in your head, you should also know that the remaining trump card is the seven. You then lead with the queen of hearts, and because West can no longer follow suit, they discard the two of clubs, at which point you play the ten of hearts from the dummy hand, and East plays the last remaining trump card. Now you no longer need to worry about any tricks being trumped by your opponents.

Most importantly, the singleton in West's cards no longer matters. Because you have captured all of the trump cards held by your opponents, you can now play your ace, king, and queen of diamonds with no worries. They have now become guaranteed winners. Also, note that if the number of trump cards in the dummy hand had been two instead of three, you could have used the final trump trick (the queen) to discard one of those low value and sure loser spade cards, thus eliminating two potential problems on one trick.

Establishing Length Winners

Another way of promoting cards is to take advantage of long suits. For example:

```
                    DUMMY
                    ♠764
        WEST                        EAST
      ♠ A102                        ♠95
                    SOUTH
                  ♠ KQJ83
```

Assume that you have now collected all of the trump cards from your opponents, and, based on the total of eight spades in your hand and in the dummy hand, you know that your opponents hold only five spades. Assume that the dummy hand is now in the lead and you would like to win a few more tricks in spades. How can you do that?

First, you play the four of spades from the dummy hand, then East plays the nine of spades, and you respond by playing the king of spades. This forces West to win the trick with the ace of spades. Your opponents now have only three spades left in their cards. Now, assuming West leads in a different Suit (e.g., clubs), you should take this trick from the cards in your hand, if possible. Now that you again have the lead, you play the queen of spades, which is a definite winner because both the ace and king have been played, and you need not worry about trump cards. West plays the two of spades, you play the six of spades from the dummy hand, and East plays the nine. Now you know that your opponents have only one spade remaining, and you should also know that it is the ten of spades. Now you lead the jack of spades, which you know—because of your promotion tactics—is now the highest spade card remaining. West is now forced to play the ten of spades, you play the seven from the dummy hand, and East (who is now void in Spades and holds no more trump cards) discards a low card in another suit.

Now you can lead with the eight of spades fully confident that it is a winner. You know that eleven of the thirteen spade cards have been played, and you have the last two in your hand. So, when you lead with the eight, neither opponent will be able to follow suit, enabling you to win the trick by default. The same will be true when you then lead with the three of spades. Three factors allowed you to promote the eight and three of spades into sure winners: the length of the suit in your hand, the order in which you took steps to eliminate trump cards, and the moves you took to eliminate the spades held by your opponents.

Winning Sure Tricks

Only after you have established and won the additional sure tricks you created and have captured all of the trump cards, should you turn your attention to your sure winners. As discussed earlier, doing this too soon can result in unexpected and undesirable surprises, so you need to be careful.

First, by playing sure winners too soon, you may actually end up promoting cards held by your opponents into winners. For example, if your side holds an ace of diamonds but not the king of diamonds, leading with the ace would not be a good strategy. Your opponent will likely just play some low card in diamonds because they know that the trick is lost; the result of this is that you have now promoted their king of diamonds into a winner. However, if you wait until an opponent leads in that suit, their partner may erroneously play the king in an attempt to win the trick, and then you can capture the king with your ace, a card that might have otherwise have won a trick for your opponents. Also, as discussed earlier, you could end up getting sure winners trumped because of unexpected voids. Consequently, you should always eliminate the trump cards held by your opponents before playing sure winners.

The Finesse

A **finesse** is, first and foremost, a tactic you can use during the playing of the cards to fool your opponent into giving you a winning trick that you might not otherwise have won. But it also involves a gamble on your part. Usually, it is done when you have some of the face cards in a suit. For example, you may have the ace and queen of clubs in your hand, and the jack and six of clubs in the dummy hand. If you just start by leading with the ace of clubs from your hand, you will certainly win that trick. But you don't have the king, and this move will promote that king to the highest remaining club and a sure winner. However, if you take a slightly different approach, you may be able to avoid that problem completely.

For example, instead of leading in clubs from your hand, get the lead to the dummy hand, and lead the six of clubs from there. Now, you know that the king of clubs is in the hands of your opponents, but you don't know which opponent holds it. After you lead with the six of clubs, East must decide what to do. If they hold the king, and they choose to play it, they know that there is a very good chance that they will lose the trick and the king because you likely hold the ace. So, they may decide hold onto the king and simply play a club that is higher than the six that you started with (e.g., the nine of clubs), hoping that you will win the trick with the ace, thus promoting their king. Of course, another possible situation is that East does not have the king and, unbeknownst to East, it is in fact held by West. Under these circumstances, East may still make exactly the same play of the nine of clubs.

Now, it is your turn as the declarer and, of course, you do not know which of your opponents holds the king. If it is held by East, playing the ace will certainly promote it. If you don't play the ace, and instead play the jack, and West actually holds the king, you will certainly lose the trick when West plays the king. But what if

East does hold the king and just chose not to play it? You think that may be the case, and so you choose to gamble (or "guess") and play the jack, believing that West will not be able to win the trick. And you are correct. West plays a low club on the the trick. And so, not only do you win the trick, but you now also know for certain that East has the king. That is a finesse. You have won a trick that you might have otherwise lost; by virtue of a game, you have perhaps gotten closer to completing your contract.

This can be an especially beneficial tactic in situations where it gets you closer to creating voids, capturing high trump cards, or taking advantage of short suits in the cards of your opponents. For example, what if the only cards in clubs East held had been the king and eight of clubs? If you had just led with the ace from your hand, you would have won that trick. But in the process, you would have promoted the king into a sure winner for your opponents. However, as a result of your finesse, East now holds a singleton king. Now when you lead with the ace, East must follow suit and play the king. Not only do you win that trick, but you have also eliminated any threat posed by the king.

Of course, a finesse can also be executed in the other direction. In other words, you could start with a low card from your hand, and then wait to see what West does next. Now, you have a higher and a lower face card in the dummy hand (e.g., an ace and a queen). If you believe that West holds the king (or other face card) of concern, but for some reason chose not to play it, you could gamble and choose to play the queen and not the ace and hopefully win the trick. If your gamble pays off, you have now executed a finesse on West.

One final comment about finessing. Although it most certainly involves a gamble, it need not be a reckless gamble. If you have been paying close attention during the auction, and perhaps even early on in the playing out of the cards, you may have picked up information that will help make that finesse an educated guess. For example, if East had offered some bid during the auction, especially if it was in the suit you are finessing, it is likely they have at good number of FCPs, and one of them is probably that worrisome king. So, with some information on which to base your guess, the riskiness of your finesse is reduced.

In summary, your goal as declarer is to win enough tricks to complete your contract. Your skills and judgment in using techniques such as card promotion, establishing voids, collecting and/or ruffing with trump cards, establishing length winners, finessing, and eventually winning tricks with high face cards, will help to determine the outcome.

Chapter 7:
Playing the Hand: No-Trump Contracts

Playing a Bridge hand for a no-trump contract is in many ways similar to playing a hand in a contract with a trump suit. Your basic approach should be no different. Take your time, review the bidding in your head, study the lead card, examine the dummy hand carefully, count your sure winners, and make a careful plan for completing your contract. However, there are some critical differences and inherent dangers in no-trump contracts that warrant special attention. Moreover, since the three no-trump contract is the most commonly played contract in Bridge, this chapter will focus on playing out the hand for that type of contract.

If you are very fortunate, as soon as you see the dummy hand, you will realize that a three no-trump contract is exactly where you should be. You count your sure tricks and you clearly have enough of them. One clear advantage of a no-trump contract is that counting sure winners is more straightforward and certain since the value of the cards is determined solely by their pip value. There will be no trump cards to complicate matters.

Consequently, if you play the hand correctly, you will easily complete your no-trump contract.

For example:

DUMMY

♠ 8 5 4

♥ 8 3

♦ A K Q J 7

♣ J 10

DECLARER

♠ A K Q 10

♥ A 9

♦ 9 8 6 4

♣ A 8 4

In this three no-trump contract situation, you have five sure winners in diamonds, three in spades, one in hearts, and one in clubs, for a total of ten.

Remember, you only need to win nine tricks for your contract.

Assuming that West leads with a low club, you should take that trick with the ace, then lead a low diamond back to the dummy hand, win the trick with the ace, and then lead with the king, queen, and jack in succession. At this point, you should have also cleared out all of the diamonds held by your opponents, so you should also be able win a trick with the seven of diamonds, because neither of your opponents will be able to follow suit. You now have won six tricks. For the final three required for your contract, lead with any of the spades back to your hand, take the trick with the ace, and then collect two more tricks in spades by leading with the king and queen. You have now won the nine tricks you needed. However, you can now also win one overtrick by leading with the ace of hearts.

As you can see, the simplicity and straightforwardness of a no-trump contract can be very appealing. Unfortunately, it isn't always quite as easy as suggested by this example. More often than not, when you count your sure winners, you will realize that you do not have enough to guarantee success at completing your contract. Consequently, you will need to be creative. As with the playing of a trump contract, you will need to establish some additional winners. The techniques by which you can do that are some of the same ones used in trump contracts (e.g., promoting cards, establishing long suits, finessing, etc.).

Promoting Cards

One of the most common techniques used to establish additional winning tricks, even in no-trump contracts, is promoting cards.

For example:

DUMMY

♠ 8 7 3

♥ A 8 4

♦ 9 6 5 2

♣ A K 2

DECLARER

♠ K Q J 10

♥ K Q 9

♦ A K 8 3

♣ 6 5

Assume that the contract is for three no-trump, and West leads with a small heart. You need to win nine total tricks. You count your sure tricks and determine that you only have seven: two in clubs, two in diamonds, and three in hearts. In order to complete your contract, you will need to somehow establish at least two more winning tricks. Using the tactic of promoting cards, you can do that quite easily. You will want to have the lead in your hand, so you play the four of hearts, and then win the trick with the queen of hearts. Now, while you still have strong stoppers in every other suit, lead with the ten of spades from your hand. Since one of your opponents clearly has the ace of spades, they will need to play it to win the trick. Once they have done that, your king, queen, and jack of spades become sure winners. And you can be absolutely certain they are winners because there is no trump suit. You gave up one trick and gained three as a result. You now have won one trick, and have nine more sure tricks.

Assume that East won the spade trick with the ace and then led with a low diamond. Take that trick with the king, then lead with the nine of hearts back to the dummy hand. Take that trick with the ace of hearts. Now, take two more tricks from the dummy hand with the ace and king of clubs. Then, lead with the remaining heart card back to your hand, and win it with the king of hearts. Now, lead with the ace of diamonds, followed by the king, queen, and jack of spades, and claim four more tricks. You win a total of ten tricks and easily make your contract of three no-trump, with one overtrick.

Sometimes, successfully establishing winners by promoting cards can have major implications.

For example:

DUMMY

♠ K83

♥ A73

♦ 874

♣ KQJ10

DECLARER

♠ AQJ5

♥ K4

♦ AKQ

♣ 8765

Assume your contract is for six no-trump. You will therefore need to win twelve tricks. You count your sure winners and determine that you have two sure tricks in hearts, four in spades, and three in diamonds, giving you a total of nine. Consequently, you will need to establish three more sure winners in order to complete your contract. West leads with the queen of hearts. If you can just get rid of the ace of clubs, you can easily establish three more tricks there. So you win the heart trick with your king, and then lead with the king of clubs. The ace of clubs is played and wins that trick. Now you have three more sure tricks. Since you have stoppers in every suit, you can easily regain the lead by winning the next trick, and then win ten more tricks in succession, completing a small slam, and scoring a lot of bonus points toward winning the rubber.

Establishing Long Suits

Another technique for establishing additional winning tricks is by taking advantage of long suits. This is an especially effective tactic in no-trump contracts because multiple small-value cards can quickly be made into sure winners.

For example:

DUMMY

♠ 72

♥ AK874

♦ 9873

♣ 43

DECLARER

♠ 954

♥ 532

♦ A105

♣ AKQ

Assume that your contract is for three no-trump, requiring you to win a total of nine tricks. At this point, you have only seven sure tricks between your hand and the dummy hand: two in hearts, three in clubs, and one each in diamonds and spades.

Somehow you need to establish two more. Notice, you don't really have any options to establish winners by promoting cards, as you did in the previous examples. The best approach to establish winners in this hand is to establish some additional winners in your longest suit. Your team holds a total of eight hearts, leaving your opponents with five. Assuming those five cards **break** so that one opponent holds two, and the other opponent holds three, you can establish two additional heart winners, for a total of four. That would give you the two additional winners you need. But how?

First, no matter what West leads with, you should win the first trick in your hand and get the lead back there as soon as possible. Then, lead with the two of hearts. You could certainly then take that trick in the dummy hand with the ace or king, and then lead with the other, and then lead with another heart (e.g., the eight). But you will certainly lose that last trick because, although you have now captured four of the five hearts held by your opponents, they still have the ten. Moreover, look carefully at what that would do to the dummy hand. You have eliminated your only **entry** back to the dummy hand, which will prevent you from ever getting the lead back there so you can lead with your two remaining trick-winning hearts.

An alternative approach would be to **duck** on the first heart trick. In other words, retain your two face cards in hearts by playing a low heart card from the dummy hand and allow your opponents to win that trick. Now, your opponents have only three hearts left and, assuming that the ten was not used to win the previous trick, it is still out there as part of a 2-1 break. But, it will now certainly be captured when you lead with the ace and king from the dummy hand, thus making your two remaining low heart cards into sure winners. So, all you have to do now is take the next trick in your hand with a stopper in whatever suit was led, and then lead back to the dummy hand with a heart, win with the ace of hearts, and then lead with the king of hearts. Now, since the ten is gone, you can also win two more heart tricks as well. Since you were able to establish two additional winning tricks in hearts because of your length in that suit, you complete your contract by winning three club tricks, one diamond trick, one spade trick, and four heart tricks.

Sometimes, you may need to establish two long suits in order to win enough tricks to complete your contract, and the order in which you establish each one can be important. As a general rule, you should focus on the weaker of the two suits first.

For example:

DUMMY

♠ QJ2

♥ K965

♦ AK73

♣ 96

DECLARER

♠ K95

♥ A1074

♦ 642

♣ AQ4

Assume that the contract is three no-trump and West leads
with the four of clubs. When you count your sure tricks, you will
find only five: two in hearts, one in clubs, and two in diamonds.
This means that you will need to somehow establish at least four
more winners in order to complete your contract.

However, if you think carefully about the lead card played by
West, you should notice something else. West has put you in a
potential finesse situation in clubs. When a defender plays
themselves into a finesse situation in this manner, it is called a

free finesse. Obviously, you will play a low club from the dummy hand. Then East may need to decide what to do. If they hold the king and choose to play it, you will win the trick with ace, thus promoting your queen as another sure winner. However, if East doesn't have the king, or ducks, you can finesse by playing the queen. If your gamble pays off, you win a trick you might otherwise have lost, thus increasing your total of winners to six instead of five. Whichever way East plays, you end up with another winner—a freebie.

So, now you only need to establish three additional tricks. Two of these tricks will come from spades, and the third will come from hearts. Consequently, you will need to establish both spades and hearts; since the weaker of the two is spades, this is where you should begin. You need to force out the ace of spades so you can promote your other remaining spade face cards. With the lead in your hand as a result of the free finesse, play the king of spades to force out the ace. If the ace is played, then your queen and jack are established as two additional winners. If the ace is not played (an opponent is ducking), lead with another spade from your hand. Assume that West finally plays the ace, wins the trick, and then leads back with another club. You should hold onto your remaining club face card (ace or queen) as a stopper for later. So, duck this trick. Then, regardless of what is led, work to get the lead back to your hand. Next, lead with the three of hearts and finesse with the nine. If this is successful, you will have gained that ninth trick you needed by making the nine of hearts into a winner.

The Finesse

As with trump contracts, finessing can be an effective way of establishing additional sure winners needed to complete a contract.

For example:

DUMMY

♠ J107

♥ AKQJ5

♦ 83

♣ 1054

DECLARER

♠ AK8

♥ 9864

♦ A9

♣ KQJ2

Assume you are the declarer in a three no-trump contract and that West leads with a low diamond card. You clearly have two sure winners in spades with the ace and the king, and one sure winner in diamonds. You will also have five sure winners in hearts, assuming there is an even break of the four missing hearts between your opponents, thus making your five of hearts also a winner. That is eight of the nine tricks that you need for your contract. Furthermore, you can establish three more tricks in clubs if you can just force out the ace. Your diamonds, however, are weak at best. Even with 17 FCPs, a relatively even distribution of suits (e.g., 2-4-3-4), and face-card points in three suits, the strength of your cards for a no-trump contract can still be shaky if a suit is weak in both your hand and the dummy hand.

Because of West's lead, you must win the first trick with the ace of diamonds, leaving you even weaker and more at risk in diamonds. Typically, when playing a no-trump contract, and with a suit as weak as this one, you simply cannot afford to lose the lead. If you try to establish the additional club tricks by now leading with one of your three face cards, your opponent will win the trick with the ace. They will then immediately play diamonds back and forth with their partner, and you will have no choice but to watch as they win trick after trick, before you can regain the lead.

A better approach would be to win the first trick with the ace of diamonds, but then lead back with the ace of spades. You may get lucky and one of your opponents may have the queen as a singleton. Then, take your five heart tricks from the dummy hand and discard the nine of diamonds in your hand on the final heart trick. It is worthless to you anyhow. Now you have won seven tricks.

What next? Why not try to win an extra trick with a finesse in spades? In fact, this is likely your only hope for winning nine tricks and completing your contract. Lead with the jack of spades from the dummy hand, and gamble that East has the queen but chose not to play it. Play the eight of spades from your hand. If the finesse works, use the king of spades to win your ninth trick. If it doesn't work, at least you will only be set back by one trick instead of four or five.

Holding the Lead

As discussed earlier, a no-trump contract is typically declared when your team holds a lot of FCPs and a relatively even distribution between the suits. However, you as declarer, and perhaps your partner, having an even distribution does not preclude the possibility that one of your opponents has a long suit. If they are able to get the lead and establish that suit—by promoting face cards into sure winners, capturing low-value face cards because they have little protection, or because of mistakes on your part—it can become a major headache in a no-trump contract. They can just keep leading in that suit, rendering even low-value cards sure winners because there are no trump cards. And so there is nothing you can do to stop it.

Consequently, if your team has any relatively weak (few FCPs) suits, or suits with only three cards, you should immediately take special notice of such situations and be extra careful so you can avoid a catastrophe.

For example:

DUMMY

♠ K4

♥ 1032

♦ J1052

♣ AK53

DECLARER

♠ A8

♥ KQJ5

♦ AK93

♣ 764

In this example, you have six sure winners: A-K of diamonds, A-K of spades, and A-K of clubs. Moreover, promoting the king, queen, and jack of hearts by driving out the ace will create three more sure winners. But you should also pay attention to your otherwise-weak spade suit. It could become a problem later on.

Also, if you can finesse out the queen of diamonds, you can promote two additional diamond cards into winners (J-10). Even if the finesse does not work, you would still promote the jack of diamonds into a winner.

Now, assume West leads in spades, you win the spade trick with the king, and then you try the diamond finesse on East by leading with either the jack or the ten. You gamble that East holds the queen and just chose not to play it. So, you play the three, but you are wrong. It doesn't work and West takes the trick with the queen. Now, West leads with a spade which forces out your ace of spades because it is the last spade in your possession. You win the trick with the ace. But now what do you do? You have no spades left, and this is a recipe for disaster if your opponents regain the lead.

You have now won only two tricks and have only five remaining sure winners (three in diamonds and two in clubs). Even if you keep the lead and play them all now, they will not get you to nine total tricks and your three no-trump contract. At some point, you will need to lead in hearts. As soon as you do that, your opponents will play the ace of hearts, take the lead from you again, and play spades back and forth with each other. You cannot do anything because you cannot follow suit, nor can you use trumps to take back the lead and stop the carnage. Your opponents will win the next five tricks, leaving you with a total of only seven tricks won and a failed contract. Too add insult to injury, you will be forced to discard what you initially counted as sure winners in hearts on spade tricks likely won with a three and a two.

What was your mistake? What could you have done differently to make your contract possible? Basically, you got greedy. You had already counted six sure tricks, and you knew you could easily create three more just by forcing out the ace of hearts to promote the K-Q-J. Any cards promoted by the finesse in diamonds would have just resulted in overtricks. Overtricks are nice, and finesses are fun, but they are not worth risking the contract. Also, you might have done better if you had timed the finesse better. In a no-trump contract, keeping the lead is very, very important, especially with few spade stoppers, which your opponents certainly knew about and knew how to exploit. Often, when you use a technique to establish additional winners, timing can be just as important as what technique you use.

An alternative approach would have been to win the opening trick with the king of spades as before, but instead of attempting the diamond finesse immediately, you drive out the ace of hearts by leading the ten from the dummy hand. Then, when you regain the lead with your ace of spades, you play out your remaining seven sure tricks (two diamonds, three hearts, and two clubs) in succession. That will give you nine tricks won and your contract. Then, and only then, would you try the finesse for the overtrick.

At times, you can afford to lose the lead to one opponent but not the other. If so, look for ways of keeping the dangerous hand off the lead.

Hold-Up Plays

Sometimes you can minimize the risk of a dangerous suit by holding onto any stopper you might have in that suit for as long as possible. This can also serve to confuse and disrupt the plans of the defenders.

For example:

```
                        DUMMY
                        ♠75
                        ♥K742
                        ♦75
                        ♣AQJ63
WEST                                              EAST
♠Q1084                                            ♠963
♥106                                              ♥QJ95
♦K10862                                           ♦QJ9
♣98                                               ♣K75


                        SOUTH
                        ♠AKJ2
                        ♥A83
                        ♦A43
                        ♣1042
```

You have six sure tricks: two in hearts, two in spades, one in diamonds, and one in clubs. Since your contract is for three no-trump, you will need to win nine tricks. You can establish another three tricks in clubs if you can finesse out the king. Normally, you might want to get this king problem solved right away. However, you should be careful. Your diamond suit is quite weak, with only one stopper, so losing the lead could create a big problem. When the opponents get the lead, they would be able to play and win enough diamond tricks to defeat your contract.

Assume that West leads with a low diamond and you win the trick with the ace of diamonds. Now, you try a finesse for the king of clubs by leading the two and then playing the queen from the dummy hand. Unfortunately, the finesse fails and East wins the trick with the king of clubs. Then they lead with the queen of diamonds, followed by another diamond. West wins that trick with the king and then leads with diamond after diamond while you helplessly watch. Your opponent will win four diamond tricks after the one club trick, and your team will win (at best) eight tricks.

What could you have done to prevent this disaster? Instead of winning the first trick with the ace of diamonds, you duck. Allow East to win the first trick by playing a low diamond from your hand—in other words, hold-up your ace. East then leads with the diamond queen just as before, but you duck once again. East then leads with a third diamond. You win that trick with the ace and then lead with the ten of clubs to try the finesse. East wins that trick also because, as before, the finesse fails. But, because of your **hold-up**, East is now out of diamonds. They must then lead in another suit where you have guaranteed entries. This allows you to regain the lead and then win nine straight tricks.

In summary, playing out a no-trump contract may be more straightforward and less unpredictable—but only if you keep your head in the game, plan carefully, and don't get careless. You should have a good reason for every card you play and the order in which you play them.

Chapter 8: Defensive Play

In the preceding two chapters, we have discussed playing out Bridge hands when your team has won the auction. But what about situations where your opponents have won the auction and you and your partner are now the defenders? Obviously, neither you nor your partner are holding particularly strong cards. There is no cause for despair. Many contracts are not completed and so there is still hope, especially if you can help your own cause by playing defense well. This is why developing your skills in this area of Bridge is just as important as learning to play any other part of the game.

First, you should keep in mind that once a rubber has been completed, it is the total number of points scored by a team that determines the winner of the rubber. Of course, the first team to win two games gets the rubber bonus, and that is usually enough to ensure they will also win the rubber on total points. However, it is not uncommon for a team to win two games and earn the rubber bonus, but still lose the rubber because their opponents scored a lot of penalty points on earlier hands. So, you should always approach defensive play with the same level of focus and care as you would the auction phase or when trying to complete a contract. Defensive play can win rubbers also.

Moreover, when on defense, you need to strike a balance between being overly passive and being cautious (as opposed to being overly aggressive and reckless). You should take only reasonable risks based on careful consideration and the best information available. The strength of your cards, the level reached in the contract, the suit of the contract, your position at the table relative to the opponent who opened the bidding, your team's vulnerability, and your team's position in the rubber should always be taken into consideration when deciding how to proceed on defense. Of course, as defenders you are also at a slight informational disadvantage. The declarer can see all of the cards held by their team. But, although both defenders can also see the dummy hand, they cannot see each other's cards. This makes effective communication between partners when on defense even more important.

Finally, you should also keep in mind that defensive tactics may differ slightly depending on whether the contract is a trump contract or a no-trump contract, and whether you are playing defense as the first defender (West) or as the second defender (East).

Defending Against a Trump Contract

Assume that North and South have won the auction and the result is a contract for four hearts. In other words, your opponents need to win ten tricks. As defenders, your goal is to win at least four tricks, leaving your opponents at least one short of their contract.

Leading

Your defense begins when your team leads with the first card to get the gameplay started. Also, at various points during the play, you likely will have other opportunities to get a trick started by leading. In any event, choosing what card to play under such circumstances is important. Take your time, review the bidding in your head, count sure winners as best you can, and make a plan for establishing additional winners, in either your hand or the cards of your partner. Remember, declarers will seldom have enough sure winners to guarantee they can complete their contract. So, part of your task will be to make sure they have difficulty establishing more.

Once you have thought through each of these issues, then (and only then) should you choose the card you will lead with. You have a variety of options, depending on the circumstances, so choose carefully.

The most common lead is a low card (e.g., a four or a three) in a non-trump suit. Usually, this will be the fourth best card that you hold in that suit. This is a safe, somewhat passive, lead. While you most certainly will lose the trick, this loss also does the least amount of damage to the cards you (and your partner) hold. You do not want to waste a potentially valuable high face card on a trick you will certainly lose, or that your partner might be able to win with a high face card or a trump card.

Another common, somewhat more aggressive lead is to open with a singleton that would immediately create a void in some suit in your cards, thus allowing you to win tricks with trump cards as soon as possible. However, it is usually not a good strategy to lead with a singleton ace if you have another lead that makes more sense. If your partner does not have the king, you would immediately establish another winner (the king) for your opponents, and it is likely all you will capture with the ace are low cards anyhow. The other team can see immediately that they will lose the trick and therefore has no incentive to play anything higher.

Leading from a doubleton might also be a smart move if your partner bid in that suit, or if you have some length in the trump suit. But you should always lead with the higher card first, so that when you play the second card, your partner knows you now have a void. Then, perhaps you can win a few tricks by ruffing. However, if you hold a doubleton of face cards, you should only lead from that suit if your partner bid in that suit, and if that doubleton is an A-K, then you should lead with the king, as a signal to your partner that you also hold the ace. You should never lead with the ace in this situation.

If you have the ace of a suit and several lower cards in the same suit, but not the king, you should never lead with one of the lower cards. **Under-leading** an unsupported ace or king (not having the next lower value face card), especially in a trump contract, is not a good tactic because it would give the declarer an easy trick. For example, if you hold the ace, ten, seven, five, and three of diamonds, and the declarer has the king, the declarer will easily win that trick. Or, if the declarer just happens to have the king as a singleton, they would win that trick and then lose no more tricks in that suit. Your ace then may become worthless because it could get beaten by a trump card. In fact, it is best not to lead from that suit at all. Hold onto the ace in case an opportunity arises later in the play to capture the king with the ace.

However, if the bidding has told you that the cards of your opponents are especially strong, and you are unsure how many tricks you can win, if any, leading with an ace, even an unsupported one, might be appropriate. Or, if you believe that your partner has been dealt (or has established) a singleton in that suit, thus creating a ruffing opportunity, leading with the ace can also be a good choice.

Another option is to lead with a low card in a suit that was bid by your partner. Or, you could lead with a middle card in the suit bid by your partner. This is a way of **signaling** to your partner that, after they win the trick, they should lead in the same suit, because you hold another high face card in that suit and can then win another trick.

Of course, if your partner offered no bids, you might choose to lead from a suit that your opponents did not bid, because your partner might have high face cards in that suit.

Another good option is to lead from a suit that has a particularly strong combination, or that has the potential to promote cards that can create one, such as A-K, K-Q-J, or Q-J-10. But, always lead with the lowest card in the sequence.

You can also lead with a trump if you have no other lead that is safe. This may prevent the declarer from using the dummy hand's trumps immediately or effectively, or insure that they are quickly depleted.

Leading from a particularly long suit (six or more) would not be a good idea, because after the trump cards have all been collected, that long suit can become extremely valuable for your team if you can manage to regain the lead. If that happens, every card you retain in that suit could result in another lost trick for your opponents. Getting the lead back from your opponents as often as possible, and maintaining it for as long as possible, is always a good defensive tactic. This is another reason why leading with an ace would be unwise. You may need the ace to regain the lead when necessary. Of course, your opponents will be trying to force you to play any aces you may hold, but as a general rule, you should try to hold on to them for as long as possible.

Some experienced Bridge players also recommend against under-leading against broken high-card combinations (e.g., A-Q-10, K-J-10, Q-10-9). However, this is somewhat controversial. Leading with a low card beneath a broken high-card combination can often establish more winning tricks by promoting the high cards held by your team before your opponents have the opportunity to capture them. Of course, by leading this way, you are also gambling on what you hope your partner holds. However, taking such a risk may often be your only hope of preventing the success of the contract. As always, when taking such a risk, make use of all of the information available to you (e.g., the history of the auction, previous cards played by your partner, etc.).

Finally, when leading, you should be decisive. Any apparent indecision on your part may be seen by the declarer as information about what you're holding in a suit. Try to decide in advance which card you're going to play when the declarer leads to or from the dummy, and then play it without hesitation.

Responding to Your Partner's Lead

Your partner has made the lead, the dummy's hand has been revealed, and the declarer has played a card on the trick from the dummy's hand. As the **third hand,** it's now your turn to play. At this point, you have a lot of information available to you. You have heard the bidding, you have seen your partner's opening lead, and you've seen the dummy's hand. So, what do you do now?

There is an old and common expression in Bridge: "Second Hand Low, Third Hand High." This basically means that when on defense, the type of card you play on a trick depends on where you are seated relative to the lead. However, this is often an oversimplification because there is another popular admonition that instructs that you should "cover an Honor with an Honor." These expressions are not contradictory; in fact, both are good advice.

When the declarer wins a trick from either their hand or the dummy's hand, they must then lead for the next trick. Thus, they become the **first hand**. If you are the first player to play after such a lead, you are then the **second hand.** If the lead was a low card, you should also play a low card (second hand low), preferably under the value of the card led. The goal is to force the third hand (declarer or dummy) to play a high card, so then the fourth hand (your partner) has an opportunity to capture that trick with an even higher card. However, if the lead was a high card (e.g., a jack), you should play a higher-value card such as a queen (cover an honor with an honor).

If you are the third hand responding to a low-value card led by your partner and a low card played from the dummy's hand, you should probably the play a high card. You do not want to give the opponents a cheap trick, which would likely happen if you also played a low card. Even if a high card is played from the dummy's hand, you should still play a higher card, if possible, to force an even higher card to be played by the **fourth hand** (declarer). In other words, if you have the jack, eight, seven, and five, then play the jack. If you have the king, eight, and three, then play the king.

Moreover, when you are a third hand holding the ace of a suit, you should play it (most of the time). For example, assume that your partner leads with the four of clubs and the dummy hand (holding the ten, six, and two of clubs) plays the two. If you have the ace, queen, and three of clubs, then you should play the ace. Even if your partner leads with a face card like a queen or a jack and the dummy hand plays a low card, you should still play the ace.

The only time this rule does not apply is if you have touching face cards, such as A-K or K-Q. Under these circumstances, you still play "high," but with the lower-valued card of the touching pair (e.g. king or queen), respectively. If you have a long touching sequence, such as K-Q-J-10-9, you should play the nine.

However, under certain unusual circumstances, it may be appropriate to play a low card as the third hand.

For example,

DUMMY
♦KJ4

WEST   EAST
♦10865   ♦Q92

SOUTH
♦A73

With some other suit as trump, West leads the ten of diamonds, which typically indicates that they hold no cards higher than the ten. Then the dummy hand plays the four of diamonds, and you know your partner does not have the ace (because your partner would not under-lead an ace). Under these circumstances, it is a better tactic to save your queen (in order to possibly capture the jack from the dummy hand) and play the nine instead. It is not necessary to play high in this situation. All of the cards higher than your nine have been accounted for, and so the nine will be sufficient to drive out the ace.

Signaling

As defenders, it is entirely acceptable for you and your partner to communicate with each other based on the cards you choose to play, or the order in which you play them, and you should do so whenever possible. In fact, signaling in this manner is an important defensive skill in Bridge.

There are many kinds of signals that may be communicated. A few of the more common ones are **attitude signals**, **count signals**, and **suit-preference signals.** Moreover, these signals can be arranged in a hierarchy of interpretation preference. In other words, any signal should be assumed to be an attitude signal, unless that would not make sense under the circumstances. Then, it should be considered a count signal, unless that does not make sense either. Only as a last resort, should it be interpreted as a suit-preference signal. Another complicating factor is that there are basically two conventions for the use of signals—standard signals and upside-down signals. In this book, we will primarily discuss the standard convention. However, Bridge partners should discuss this issue in advance of playing so they can agree on which convention to use, and of course, they should also then disclose their chosen convention to their opponents.

Attitude Signals

One group of signals is intended to either encourage or discourage certain actions by your partner. For example, you may want to encourage your partner to lead in a particular suit, or conversely, discourage them from leading in a particular suit. Such signals can be sent in a variety of ways, and usually involve only the cards from two to nine.

Leads. One method of attitude signaling is by the card you choose when you have the lead. As discussed earlier, leading with a medium or higher card can signal that you like a particular suit, and thus suggest that your partner lead it back to you as soon as possible. Or, leading with a low card could indicate there is nothing special about the cards you hold in this suit and so your team should try a different one. However, you could also use the **BOSTON lead signals** convention, which is an upside-down approach to encouragement or discouragement. BOSTON does not actually refer to the city. It is an acronym that stands for "Bottom Of Something, Top Of Nothing." With this convention, if you lead low, you are telling your partner that you have some pretty good high cards in this suit. But if you lead with a high card, you are saying that you have little strength in this suit, so switch to another one.

Cards played. Another common method of attitude signaling is by playing certain cards in certain circumstances. In other words, the cards you choose to play, and when you play them, communicates your attitude to your partner.

For example:

WEST

♣A 9 4 2

EAST

♣K 8 5 3

Assume that you are East, your partner leads with the ace of clubs, and you play the three on that trick. You know you can win another trick with the king, and so you want to encourage your partner to lead the same suit back to you. But your partner doesn't know you have the king, and may therefore lead back in a different Suit. Normally, you might be inclined to play your lowest-value club card on the ace trick. Of course, your partner knows that also. In keeping with the standard model of attitude signaling, you should play the eight of clubs instead of the three. Playing a higher-value card in a situation where a low-value card would be expected is a way of signaling to your partner that they should continue in the same suit and lead it back to you. In contrast, the upside-down convention for signaling would require that you encourage your partner by playing a low card and discourage them by playing a high card.

A similar situation may be when you have a doubleton in a particular suit and the dummy hand has at least three cards in that suit. As mentioned earlier, if your partner leads with a king in that suit, they are telling you that they also hold the ace. After your partner wins that trick, you want to encourage them to now lead with the ace, so you can create a void in your hand that might allow you to win another trick with a trump card later on. But, how do you let your partner know that?

Play the highest card from the doubleton. For example, if you have a nine and a two, you would play the nine. Because that is a higher-value card, as discussed earlier, you have signaled to your partner to lead with the same suit again (according to the standard model of signaling). Since your partner knows that you know they also hold the ace (you were told that earlier when they led with the king), they will interpret your signal as indicating that you want them to now lead with the ace, so you can be assured of winning the trick. When you play the two on the next trick, your partner will know that you probably now have a void in that suit, because you played high and then low. They will then lead with the same suit again, so you can win that trick by ruffing. The result is that your team has won a trick that you might otherwise have lost, and that one trick may be the one that prevents your opponents from completing their contract.

Discards. You can also communicate attitude signals to your partner by what cards you choose to discard under certain circumstances. Normally, when you discard, you would discard the lowest-value card possible. So, when you instead discard a middle or high-level card, you can communicate to your partner that you like this suit for some reason, and they should lead it back to you. You can also signal the creation of a void by discarding high and then low in a suit, especially if you are discarding from a doubleton.

Count Signals

Count signals are used to communicate the number of cards that a defender holds in a particular suit. Typically, this is communicated by the order in which cards are played or discarded. Playing or discarding high and then low in a suit indicates an even number of cards in that suit, while playing or discarding low to high indicates an odd number. Count signals can be used when either partner or declarer leads the suit.

Suit-Preference Signals

A suit-preference signal is used when either leading or following suit. For example, if you have a void in hearts, and you would like your partner to lead back to you in hearts, lead with a low card in spades. By leading with a low card in a major suit, you are telling your partner to lead you back to the lower-ranked of the the two major suits. If you want a lead back to spades, then lead with a high card in hearts. Of course, you can use the same tactic for minor suits.

The Rule of 11

The Rule of 11 is a mathematical calculation based on the assumption that your partner on defense has led with their fourth-best card in any non trump suit. The rule works because you know that your partner has exactly three cards higher than the one led, and also, the number of cards lower in rank to that card is known. For example, if the lead is a four, there are only two cards lower in value (3 and 2). The rule allows the third hand player to estimate how many cards the declarer holds in their hand that are higher than the opening lead card. To obtain the estimate, subtract the value of the opening lead card from eleven. Then count the number of cards in the dummy hand that are higher in value than the lead card and subtract that number from the previous result. Finally, subtract the number of cards in your own hand that are higher than the card led. The final number is an estimate of how many cards are in the declarer's hand that are higher in value than the lead card.

For example:

DUMMY
♠Q82

WEST   EAST
♠KJ973   ♠A105

SOUTH
♠64

Assume you partner leads with the seven of spades. Assume also that this is their fourth-best card in spades. Subtract seven from eleven and you get four. The dummy hand contains only two spades higher than seven, so you subtract two from four, resulting in two. In your hand, you also hold two spades that are higher than the seven led by your partner. You then subtract two from two and you get zero. Thus, as the third hand, you now know that the declarer holds no cards higher in value than the seven led by your partner. You also know that if the dummy hand covers that trick with the eight, the trick can be easily won with the ten. Without making this calculation, the third hand player might have played low, erroneously thinking that the declarer might have the king, jack, or nine. Finally, as the third hand player, you also now know that the king, jack, and nine are definitely held by your partner.

However, because your opponents can make the same calculation, they also know what you know. For this reason, some Bridge partners work out a modification to the Rule of 11 between them (e.g., their partner will lead with their third-best card in the suit, rather than the fourth, with the calculation then adjusted accordingly).

Defending Against a No-Trump Contract

Assume that North and South have won the auction and the result is a contract for three no-trump. Therefore, they need to win nine tricks in order to complete their contract. As defenders, the goal of your team is to win at least five tricks, leaving your opponents at least one short of their contract. Many of the same issues discussed with regard to defending against trump contracts are relevant here as well. For example, types of leads, methods of signaling, and the Rule of 11 all still apply. However, there are also some important differences in defending against no-trump contracts that you should keep in mind.

Leading

When defending against a no-trump contract, aggressiveness becomes more important, and your strongest weapon can be the long suit. Therefore, the most important thing you should try to do with the lead is establish winning tricks in your long suit as soon as possible. The general rule is to lead with the fourth-best card in your longest and strongest suit.

If you don't have a long suit, leading in a suit bid by your partner is a good strategy also. Leading in an unbid suit is also worth considering.

For example:

Your cards: ♠ 85 ♥ AJ107 ♦ 73 ♣ K10974

In this case, lead from your longest sand strongest suit, which is clubs in this case. Start out with the seven of clubs, which is the fourth card of your longest suit. Hold onto your ace of hearts so when your opponents lead in that suit, you can capture the lead and run your club suit.

Your cards: ♠ 6532 ♥10853 ♦ KQJ10 ♣ 9

Your only hope for winning tricks with this hand is to lead with the top of a sequence of touching honors. Lead with the king of diamonds. If your partner can win the trick with the ace, they will lead back to you in diamonds, and you can then win three more tricks for your side.

However, there are certain leads you might make against a trump contract that you should never make against a no-trump contract. Never lead in a suit that either of your opponents has bid. They likely have most of the high face cards in those suits, and so you would be giving them easy tricks. Also, never lead a singleton against a no-trump contract. That likely will help the declarer establish a long suit. In fact, whenever you hold a short suit against a no-trump contract, you should probably always assume that at least one of your opponents is also long in the same suit.

Play After the Lead

When defending against a no-trump contract, coordination and effective communication between you and your partner become even more important. Don't try to defeat the contract on your own. Also, the Rule of 11 becomes even more important in no-trump contracts because you have four suits to follow.

The only way to defeat a no-trump is to work together as partners.

First, you should be working together to do whatever you can do to interfere with the declarer's efforts to establish additional sure winners by promoting lower cards in any long suits they may hold. For example, by ducking on early tricks and/or by holding high face cards until you have no choice but to play them, you can often disrupt their plans enough to squeeze out one more winner for your team. At the same time, you should both also be working to establish any long suits your team has by driving out any stoppers in those suits the declarer may hold. Also, the Rule of 11 becomes even more important in no-trump contracts because you have four suits to follow. Playing out no-trump contracts often involves a race between the declarer and the defenders to establish extra winning tricks.

Secondly, a good strategy is to continue leading back and forth between you and your partner in the suit of your opening lead, especially if you and your partner hold at least seven cards in that suit. In fact, you should lead in that suit at least three times. The goal is to establish, and win, an extra trick on the fourth round of play in that suit, because there is a very good chance that one or the other of you will have greater length in that suit than either the declarer or the dummy. You can then lead with that extra card and win the trick because your opponents can no longer follow suit.

However, if your team holds only six cards in a suit, taking the suit to a fourth round of play is unlikely to establish a winner. So, a better strategy is to switch suits often, especially if you realize that continuing to lead in a particular suit will be counterproductive. In fact, when it seems likely that your opponents will win a fourth-round trick in the suit led by your team, you should immediately switch to a different suit. You should also switch suits when you are able to determine that your opponents have greater length in that suit than your team, or when the dummy hand shows length in the suit your team led.

In summary, playing out a Bridge hand on defense is just as challenging as playing out a hand to complete a contract.

Developing your skills in this aspect of the game, especially the communication and coordination between you and your partner, can help you win rubbers more often.

Chapter 9:
Advanced Concepts

While this book has discussed nearly all the basics of playing Bridge, there are a few advanced concepts that it may be helpful for you to also know something about. I will briefly discuss those topics in this chapter.

Bidding and Playing Slam Contracts

When you and your partner discover that you have really, really, good cards, you may want to consider bidding to the six level in some suit or no-trump (a small slam) or even the seven level (a grand slam). This is always a very risky endeavor. You are committing to win at least twelve of the thirteen tricks, perhaps even all thirteen of them, and that can be extremely difficult to achieve. This is why bidding to slam level is quite rare in Bridge, and successfully completing a contract at a slam level is even rarer. In fact, it has been estimated that only about 10 percent of the Bridge hands played by experienced Bridge players are for small-slam contracts, and only around 3 percent of the hands are for grand-slam contracts. Moreover, even experienced players only successfully complete their slam contracts just over a third of the time. This means that only about one out of every one hundred Bridge hands results in a successfully completed grand-slam contract. Consequently, when you can pull it off, the feeling of accomplishment can be quite gratifying, no matter what your level of experience.

You should never contemplate a possible slam contract unless you can be confident that your team holds cards worth 31 to 33 points. And, if you are contemplating a grand slam, you should be holding cards worth 35 to 37 points. These guidelines apply regardless of whether the trump is in a major suit or a minor suit. If your contract is to be no-trump, you should proceed only if the points held by your team are on the higher end of these ranges. For example, if you have cards worth 20 or more points, and your partner opens the bidding, indicating cards worth at least 13 points, this would be the time to begin considering a slam contract. You may be able to succeed in a trump suit with fewer than 31 points if you hold a rather long suit (at least an eight-card fit) of trump cards, or any long suit in a no-trump contract. Each extra trump card, or card in a long suit over eight, can usually be counted on as a sure winner. Voids, singletons, and doubletons can often also provide extra winning tricks by allowing you to ruff. Also, in a no-trump contract, any number of cards beyond six in any suit (or, even better, in two suits) can be extremely helpful in completing a slam.

However, for relatively inexperienced players, erring on the side of caution makes more sense. So, if you don't have at least 33 points (for a small slam) or 37 points (for a grand slam), don't even try. You also should probably not even consider exploring a possible slam contract unless you hold at least two aces in your cards. Finally, if you have two or more sure losers, going to a slam level would be a very bad idea. The chances of success are quite low.

Conventions

As discussed earlier, when you make a bid in Bridge, that bid can be either natural or artificial. A natural bid communicates exactly what it seems to communicate. For example, if you bid four hearts, you are proposing to complete a contract with hearts as the trump suit and you are promising to win ten tricks. Similarly, a natural penalty double expresses your belief that you can prevent your opponents from completing their contract. However, an artificial bid either communicates or requests information between team members by means of a pre-established code or convention (e.g., the Stayman convention,

Jacoby transfer, takeout double, or signaling, as discussed in earlier chapters).

Conventions are valuable in Bridge because they reduce the risk involved in certain high-risk actions or endeavors that a team might wish to pursue at various points during the game. More specifically, they can help partners find the best suit match in the cards they hold, use the bidding space more efficiently, determine the best level at which to stop bidding, and (when on defense) convey important information about what cards to play and when. Another very common use of conventions not previously discussed occurs during the auction phase of a Bridge hand as a team explores the possibility of bidding for a slam contract.

The Blackwood Convention

If, during a competitive auction, your opponents have bid four hearts, an overcall of four no-trump would normally be interpreted as a natural bid, expressing the team's full intention of settling and playing out a contract of four no-trump and trying to win ten tricks. However, a bid of four no-trump would typically be unnecessary (and quite rare) in Bridge auctions since a three no-trump contract, when completed, would be enough to win a game. However, if the partners have agreed in advance (and also informed their opponents) that they will be using the Blackwood convention, a bid of four no-trump has an entirely different meaning. Once you and your partner have exchanged enough information to allow you to find the best trump suit fit between the two of you, a bid of four no-trump communicates an **invitation to slam** to your partner —in other words, you wish to explore the possibility of bidding to a slam contract. Moreover, it requests some important information from your partner about control over various suits that will be needed in order to accurately assess the risk of pursuing the slam contract idea (e.g., the number of aces they hold).

Your partner should then respond with a level five bid that shows the exact number of aces in their hand.

The possible responses are:

5♣= 0 or 4 Aces

5♦= 1 Ace

5♥= 2 Aces

5♠= 3 Aces

As was discussed earlier, you should never even consider bidding up to a slam-level contract unless you hold at least two aces. To win twelve tricks and complete a successful small-slam contract, you will need at least three aces in the cards held by you and your partner. For a grand-slam contract, you should hold all four of the aces. So, if you have two aces, and your partner's response is five clubs, you will immediately know that they are saying "no aces" (rather than four) because you hold two of them. That means that your opponents hold the other two aces, so even a small-slam contract is a bad idea. At that point, you should issue a sign-off bid to let your partner know that you have determined that you should not go any further than the five level. If your agreed upon trump suit is hearts or spades, then bid five hearts or five spades. This tells your partner to stop there and pass. If your best trump suit is clubs or diamonds, you should bid five spades, so you don't have to go up to the six level to stay in your trump suit. This also tells your partner to respond with a bid of five no-trump, at which point you will pass and then play out a five no-trump contract.

However, if in response to your four no-trump query, your partner responds with five diamonds, you can conclude that you are missing only one ace. At that point, you should bid at the six

177

level in your trump suit, or even bid six no-trump under certain conditions. You are then on the path to completing a small-slam contract, winning twelve of the thirteen tricks, winning a game, and being rewarded with a small-slam bonus of 500 points.

If your partner responds with five hearts, you are very fortunate. You now know that your team holds all four aces. Now you can, and should, begin thinking about the possibility of a grand-slam contract, winning all thirteen tricks, winning a game, and gaining a 750-point grand-slam bonus.

But, before you decide to take such a risky step, you should get some additional information from your partner regarding the number of kings they hold. The four kings can also be important for maintaining control of all four suits. After your partner's response of five hearts, according to the Blackwood convention, you would then bid five no-trump. This bid not only informs your partner that you have determined that your team holds all four of the aces, but now asks your partner to communicate back to you how many kings they hold. In a similar fashion as before, your partner will then respond at level six accordingly.

6♣= 0 or 4 Kings

6♦= 1 King

6♥= 2 Kings

6♠= 3 Kings

If you determine that you are missing one or two kings, sign off at the six level in your trump suit if it is possible, or at six no-trump if it is not possible. However, if you discover that your team not only holds all of the aces, but also all of the Kings, bid seven in your trump suit, or bid seven no-trump, and take a shot at a grand slam.

There are some circumstances when using the Blackwood convention is not a good idea. If you have a void in some suit, a suit with only low face cards (e.g., queens or jacks, or no face cards), or your best trump suit is spades, which cuts down on the bidding space, you should forego the idea of using Blackwood, and probably also forego the idea of a slam contract altogether.

As a side note, there is a variant of the Blackwood convention (called the Roman Key Card Blackwood) that typically also attempts to account for the location of the king and/or queen of the chosen trump suit. They can often be treated as additional effective cards for controlling the trump suit.

Blackwood is a very useful tool for experienced Bridge players, but bidding to and playing out a slam-level contract is still a risky endeavor. Using the Blackwood convention, or any other convention, does not guarantee success. It simply reduces the risk somewhat by providing you with more information. You should always be prepared for the unexpected (e.g., an opponent holding two singletons, a misplay by the declarer, and so on).

The Gerber Convention

The Gerber convention is also used when contemplating a possible slam contract, and it is used to request some of the same information as the Blackwood convention. However, it is typically used when the partner has opened one no-trump or two no-trump, and so it is most likely to be used when bidding to slam level in no-trump. To request info about aces, for example, the player would not jump to four no-trump, which has a different meaning in this convention. Instead, a jump to four clubs directly from a partner's one no-trump or two no-trump bid is an artificial bid that asks about aces held by your partner. Your partner then responds as follows.

4♦ = 0 or all four Aces in hand

4♥ = 1 Ace

4♠ = 2 Aces

4NT = 3 Aces

If you determine that your team holds all four aces and you want to pursue a grand-slam contract in no-trump, a five-clubs bid then assures your partner that you have all four aces and thus asks about kings, just like the five no-trump bid after four no-trump with the Blackwood convention. Then your partner would reply at level five in the same manner to indicate how many kings they hold (e.g., five diamonds to indicate none or four kings, five hearts to indicate one, etc.).

As with Blackwood, you should not use Gerber if you have a void or a doubleton in a suit that was not bid by either team. However, because the Blackwood convention and the Gerber convention are each used under different circumstances, they are not incompatible with each other. So, it is possible that experienced Bridge players could use both conventions in the same rubber, or for different hands of the same game.

Cross-ruffing

One of the most effective tactics in playing out a Bridge hand in a trump suit is **cross-ruffing.** It is especially useful in situations where your team is missing some of the higher-value face cards in the trump suit. The goal is to make winners out of the lower trump cards despite the missing face cards.

As discussed before, ruffing is winning a trick in a non-trump suit with a trump card because of a void in that suit. A cross-ruff is a play where several tricks are won in succession by alternately ruffing from both the declarer's cards and the dummy's hand. In order to execute a cross-ruff sequence, it first has to be set up in one or both of the hands of the declarer or dummy by creating voids. Consequently, a cross-ruff requires that each partner have a non- trump short suit with corresponding length in that suit in the partner's cards. A cross-ruff also works best when both partners have an equal number of trump cards. The execution of a cross-ruff is fairly simple as this extreme example demonstrates:

DUMMY

♠ Q109762

♥ -

♦ 9876543

♣ -

SOUTH

♠ AJ8543

♥ -

♦ -

♣ 9876543

The declarer begins by playing the ace of spades, which draws out the missing king of spades, which is the only trump card not held by North-South. Then dummy plays the two of spades, and East discards the two of clubs. The declarer has won one trick.

Then, with the lead, South leads with the three of clubs, West follows suit with the ten of clubs, the declarer plays the six of spades from the dummy's hand, and East, who also must follow suit, plays the jack of clubs. The declarer has now won two tricks.

Now, the dummy leads with the three of diamonds, East plays the ten of diamonds, the declarer plays the three of spades from their hand, and then West follows by playing the two of diamonds. The declarer has now won three tricks

Next, South leads with the four of clubs, West plays the queen of clubs, the dummy plays the seven of spades, and East plays the king of clubs. The declarer has now won four tricks.
Next, the Dummy leads with the four of diamonds, East plays the jack of diamonds, South plays the four of spades, and West follows with the queen of diamonds. The declarer has now won the sixth trick.

Then, South leads with the five of clubs, West follows suit with the ace of clubs, the dummy plays the nine of spades, and East plays the ace of clubs. The declarer has now won seven tricks.

Next, the dummy leads with the five of diamonds, East plays the king of diamonds, South plays the five of spades, and West has no choice but to play the ace of diamonds. The declarer wins the eighth trick.

Now South leads with the six of clubs, West can no longer follow suit and so discards a low heart, the dummy plays the ten of spades, and East discards a low heart. The declarer has now won nine tricks.

The dummy now has one remaining trump card (queen) and four diamonds (9-8-7-6). South has only the jack of spades and eight of spades remaining in trumps, and three clubs. Since there are no more trump cards in the hands of East and West, and because the diamonds and clubs remaining are also the highest remaining cards in those two suits, the declarer can simply claim these four tricks as certain winners as well.

At this point, the declarer has completed a grand-slam contract, and won all thirteen tricks, despite having face cards worth only seven points. However, the two very fortuitous voids in diamonds and clubs held by the declarer and dummy (as well as their combined holding of twelve of the thirteen trumps), and their ability to exploit these conditions by setting up a cross-ruffing situation and playing it out successfully, is really what made the grand slam possible.

Of course, not all potential cross-ruffing situations will be this clear-cut or as easily executed, and they certainly will not always result in a completed slam contract. Double voids are extremely rare in Bridge. However, situations where a few extra tricks might be won this way are not uncommon.

In such situations, the declarer should begin by playing out all side-suit sure winners, and also collecting all trumps from opponents, before executing the cross-ruffing tactic. Without playing sure winners first, opponents may discard in the side-suits, creating voids, and thus allowing them to trump the winners later. Also, if trump cards remain in the hands of opponents, and they are able to create voids in the same suit as the declaring team, they may be able to overtrump by playing higher trump cards on tricks ruffed by the declarer.

Of course, the obvious defense against cross-ruffing is to lead in the trump suit. Forcing the declarer to waste valuable trump cards on trump tricks cuts down on the number of trump cards available for potential cross-ruffing. Although leading with trumps is not necessarily a good strategy in most situations, it can be especially effective as a defensive tactic when a potential cross-ruffing situation is identified.

Chapter 10:
Final Thoughts

There are many different ways to learn to play Bridge. I hope that this book has at least started you out in the right direction. Of course, the best teacher going forward will be experience. You should play Bridge as often as you can with real people, with friends or family, as part of a local Bridge club, or by taking Bridge classes either in person or online. If that is not possible, then the next best option would be to use some type of Bridge software or mobile device Bridge game application. Of course, there are also other ways to learn. You can practice on your own, watch Bridge-related TV shows or videos on YouTube, read Bridge articles in newspapers or magazines, read about the game on Bridge-related websites, or even read additional books.

Bridge Clubs

Rest assured, you are not alone in having difficulty rounding up three other people with the time, knowledge, and desire to spend a few hours at a Bridge table. That is why there are few places in the world without one or more Bridge clubs nearby. Just search your local telephone book or online directory and you will likely find several such groups that most certainly would welcome your involvement. You can develop your skills, make new friends, and have some fun. I once heard a story about a young woman at a Bridge club who, while playing a rubber with three other club members, looked at her watch and announced, "I'm sorry to have to break up this very pleasant game, but I'm getting married in half an hour."

Bridge clubs typically have many members with varying levels of experience. They may even allow you to just watch Bridge games as a "kibitzer," if that is how you prefer to get started, as long as you follow a few basic rules.

Watch the entire hand (don't leave in the middle of it), and do not move from one player to another during the same hand. As we have discussed throughout this book, effective Bridge play requires focus and care, so respect the players by never creating distractions. Also, do not make any comments. If a player says something to you, it is acceptable to reply; otherwise, your silence is expected. Definitely avoid showing any reactions or emotions.

Playing Online

There are several websites on the Internet that provide opportunities to play Bridge with—and—against real people in remote locations (even other countries). And since Bridge in some ways is a universal language, you may even be able to enjoy playing with people who do not even speak your language.

Software and Apps

There are numerous Bridge computer software programs available, and you can easily download a Bridge app to your phone and play at your convenience (e.g., during breaks at work, while waiting for someone, or before you go to bed).

Classes

If you feel uncomfortable playing Bridge until you have gained more knowledge about the game, you may want to take some Bridge classes or hire a private Bridge tutor. One of the best ways to find out about such opportunities is through local Bridge clubs. There are also now several Bridge training websites on the Internet and hundreds of training videos on YouTube, as well as many software and mobile apps that provide lessons.

Double Dummy

To gain practice at the bidding and playing of a Bridge hand, there is no need for other players. You can just play double dummy by yourself. Deal the cards to yourself and three other imaginary players. Then, turn all of the cards faceup, and after carefully examining each set of cards, determine what each player would bid, what would be the final contract, what would be the opening lead, and how, if you were a declarer, you would play out the hand. Then, play the hand trick by trick. If you carefully follow the guidelines presented in this book for bidding, offensive play, and defensive play, you should be able to do this honestly and productively. Decide what you actually would do in each situation if you did not know what cards were held by your partner or opponents. Most importantly, carefully consider what you would do during both the auction and playing of the hand, both as the declarer and defenders, to get more information. You may even want to try repeating the play of the hand by making small changes in the card distribution. For example, move the queen from the declarer's hand to the dummy's hand, change the number of face cards or trump cards held by each defender, etc., and see how your game will change and how many tricks you can win.

Reading

Of course, you can also learn a lot about Bridge by reading more about the game and about various concepts, techniques, tactics, and conventions not covered in this book. There are regular columns about Bridge published in most major newspapers that present you with a sample hand and typically also provide a lesson on how to deal with a particular situation you may encounter. There are also several Bridge-related magazines that you may be able to find at your local newsstand. Of course, there are also a lot of Bridge-related websites on the Internet, Including the main websites for national and international Bridge player associations and organizations (e.g., The World Bridge Federation) with which you may want to become familiar. There are also many high-quality books that have been written about Bridge for players at all skill levels. Of course, reading and practicing, do not have to be separate activities. Keep a deck of cards with your favorite book on Bridge, and use it to translate the diagramed hands of the book into "real" bridge hands. Deal the cards to match the example in the book and play it on the tabletop next to the open book. Replay as many times as you like until you understand the principle or technique.

Tournaments

Once you have gained sufficient experience and discover that you enjoy the thrill of being at the Bridge table with high stakes, you may be ready to make your first entry into a Bridge tournament. You can even work into the tournament experience gradually, if you prefer. At many tournaments, including major championships, kibitzers are often allowed, and you might even be able to volunteer as a game recorder or monitor.

Conclusion

No matter how much you learn, Bridge can never be completely mastered, and that is one aspect of the game that makes it so compelling. Moreover, no matter your age, physical condition, level of experience, or psychological state, playing Bridge can provide you with many hours of relaxation, distraction, mental stimulation and challenge, entertainment, meaningful social interaction, gratifying teamwork, and just plain fun. Bridge truly is "the game for a lifetime."

Appendix 1:
Contract Bridge Scoring System

POINTS BELOW THE LINE

TRICK POINTS (scored by the declarer)

Each odd trick in ♣ or ♦	20 points
Each odd trick in ♥ or ♠	30 points
First odd trick in NT	40 points
Subsequent odd tricks, NT	30 points
Doubled:	Multiply trick score by 2
Redoubled:	Multiply trick score by 4

POINTS ABOVE THE LINE

OVERTRICK POINTS (scored by the declarer)

Each trick over the contract in ♣ or ♦, undoubled	20 points
Each trick over contract in NT, ♥ or ♠, undoubled	30 points
Each trick over contract in any suit:	
Doubled	100 (200 if vulnerable)
Redoubled	200 (100 if vulnerable)

UNDERTRICK POINTS (scored by the defenders)

Not Vulnerable:

First undertrick	50 points
First undertrick, doubled	100 points
First undertrick, redoubled	200 points
Second and third undertrick	50 points
Second and third undertrick, doubled	200 points
Second and third undertrick, redoubled	400 points
Each subsequent undertrick	50 points
Each subsequent undertrick, doubled	300 points
Each subsequent undertrick, redoubled	600 points

Vulnerable:

First undertrick	100 points
First undertrick, doubled	200 points
First undertrick, redoubled	400 points
Each subsequent undertrick	100 points
Each subsequent undertrick, doubled	300 points
Each subsequent undertrick, redoubled	600 points

FOR THE INSULT PENALTY	50 points

BONUS POINTS (Scored by the declarers)

Doubled contract	50 points
Redoubled contract	100 points
Small slam (6 odd tricks)	500 points
(750 if vulnerable)	
Grand slam (7 odd tricks)	1,000points
(1,500 vulnerable)	

RUBBER BONUS:

If the opponents won 1 game	500 points
If the opponents won no games	700 points

HONORS POINTS (any partnership)

Four trump honors in one hand	100 points
Five trump honors in one hand	150 points
Four aces held in one hand (NT contract)	150 points

Appendix 2:
Glossary

Above the line: Refers to the horizontal line on a Bridge scoresheet. Bonus points and penalty points won are written above that horizontal line.

Ace: The highest-ranking card in any suit, symbolized by A.

Artificial bid: A bid that does not mean what it says but rather provides information to your partner, or seeks information from your partner.

Attitude signals: Messages communicated to your partner that either encourage or discourage leads or plays in a particular suit.

Auction: The bidding phase of a Bridge hand that begins with the opening bid and ends with the contract for that hand determined and awarded to one of the two teams.

Balancing: A defensive bid aimed at keeping the auction from ending at a low level, usually based on the assumption that face-card points are fairly evenly divided between the two teams.

Balanced hand: A hand of cards that has no void or singleton suits and usually no more than one doubleton. An example of a balanced distribution of cards is 4-3-3-3, 4-4-3-2, 5-3-3-2.

Bid: A statement made during a Bridge auction that proposes the number of tricks to be won, as well as which suit will be trump suit, or that there will be no trump suit (no-trump).

Bidder: A player who makes a bid.

Bidding space: The space between the lowest possible bid during an auction (one club) and the highest possible bid during an auction (seven no-trump).

Blackwood convention: An artificial bidding convention used by a team to explore the possibility of bidding up to, and completing, a slam contract. It is initiated with a bid of four no-trump, which requests that the partner indicate by their response the number of aces they hold.

Book: The first six tricks won by the declarer. Only tricks won above the book are counted toward fulfilling the final contract.

BOSTON lead signals: An upside-down signaling convention used between partners during the playing of a Bridge hand. Leading with a low-value card encourages further play in that suit, while leading with a higher-value card discourages further play in that suit.

Break: The distribution of cards held in a particular suit between teammates.

Bridge club: A group of people who regularly meet to play Bridge, learn more about Bridge, or socialize.

Broken sequence: A combination of at least three face cards with two of them in sequence, such as A-Q-J or K-J-10.

Call: A call is anything said or done when it is a player's turn to speak during an auction, including bidding, passing, doubling, or redoubling. All bids are calls, but not all calls are bids.

Card strength: The count of the value of the face cards you are dealt plus any distribution points for voids, singletons, doubletons, or long suits.

Club: The lowest-ranking suit; the symbol for it is ♣.

Contract: The number of tricks the declaring side has committed to winning either with some suit as the trump suit, or with no trump suit. A bid becomes a contract when it is followed by three consecutive passes from the rest of the players.

Convention: An agreement between partners made before a Bridge rubber begins regarding the meaning of any artificial bids or other types of calls that might be used during the auction phase of a Bridge hand, or signals that might be used during the playing of the hand.

Count: To keep track of the cards that have been played and those that remain unplaced in each of the four suits during gameplay.

Count signals: Messages communicated between partners during the playing of a Bridge hand that indicate the length the partner holds in various suits. This is typically communicated via leads or discards.

Cross-ruffing: A tactic used during the playing out of a Bridge hand in which voids are created in two different suits, one each in opposite hands. Multiple consecutive tricks are then won by leading to one hand in the suit that is void in that hand, and then winning that trick with a trump card. Then, leading back to the opposite hand in the suit in which it has a void, and winning that trick with a trump card, and so on.

Cue-bid: A type of artificial bid that is in the same suit bid by an opponent. For example, if you bid two hearts immediately after a bid of one heart by an opponent, that is a cue-bid. It communicates at least 8 points, at least five cards in two different suits, and requests that your partner respond by bidding at the next possible level in their best suit.

Cut: Splitting a deck of playing cards into two stacks of relative equal height and then placing the stack that was originally the bottom half of the deck on top of the stack that was originally the top half of the deck.

Deal: To distribute all fifty-two cards evenly between the four players, resulting in a hand of thirteen cards for each player.

Dealer: The player who distributes the cards between the players, and who is the first to make a call in the auction.

Declarer: The declarer is the player whose bid has been accepted as the contract for the hand. As the declarer, you will play out both your cards and those of the dummy, as you attempt to win enough tricks to complete the contract.

Defenders: The defenders are the players on the team that did not win the auction; they are attempting to stop the declaring team from completing their contract.

Defensive Points: Points scored as a result of penalties imposed on the declarers for failure to complete their contract.

Diamond: The third-highest suit in rank; the symbol for it is ♦.

Discard: A card you play on a trick when you are not able to follow suit with the card that was led, or choose not to play a trump card.

Distribution: The way the cards in a given suit are spread among the four players.

Distribution points: When evaluating the strength of the cards you were dealt, points can be counted for doubletons, singletons, voids, and extra long suits. These points are then added to your face-card points to get you to a combined total point count and an assessment of card strength. Distribution points are not included in this assessment if the contract is no-trump.

Double: A call that challenges an opponent's bid. It doubles the number of game points they will get if they are successful, or the number of penalty points you will get if they do not complete their contract

Double dummy: A way of practicing Bridge play without any other actual players. Cards are dealt to yourself and three imaginary players, but then all hands are placed faceup on the table. The auction and play of the hand proceeds with you playing the role of all four players.

Doubleton: Two cards only in a particular suit.

Double-jump to game: An artificial response to an opening bid at the one level in some suit that tells your partner that you have very good length in a suit, and an unbalanced hand with at least one singleton or a void. A response of four hearts to an opening bid of one heart would be a double jump to game.

Duck: To intentionally lose a trick by playing a low-value card. This may be done to establish or promote other cards into sure winners.

Dummy: The dummy is both the declarer's partner and the cards they hold. After the auction has been completed and the lead card has been played by the defender to the left of the declarer, the declarer's partner places their cards faceup on the table sorted by suit, and then these cards are played only by the declarer for that particular hand. The declarer's partner can only watch at this point, and their cards are referred to as the dummy.

Entry: A card that will guarantee the winning of a trick in a hand so that the lead can be regained for that hand.

Establishing: To make a suit or a card into sure winners, as in forcing out the ace and king in a suit to make the queen and jack (or other cards in that suit) into sure winners.

Face cards: The four highest-value cards in any suit: ace, king, queen, and jack. Also referred to as honor cards.

Face-card points (FCPs): Points assigned when evaluating the strength of cards based on face cards held: 4 points for each ace, 3 points for each king, 2 points for each queen, and 1 point for each jack. These points are then added to your distribution points, resulting in a total point count.

Finesse: An attempt to win a trick by gambling that a particular face card is located in the hand of a player who has already played a card on a trick, thus allowing you to win the trick with a lower-value card that otherwise might not have been a winner.

First hand: The player who leads, either immediately to the left of the declarer on the first trick, or on subsequent tricks as a result of having won the previous trick.

Forcing: An artificial bid given in response to an opening bid of one no-trump that discourages your partner from continuing the pursuit of a no-trump contract. It is typically executed by a jump-bid to three of any suit.

Fourth hand: The fourth and final player to play a card on a trick.

Free finesse: A finesse situation set up for a declarer by the card that was led by an opponent.

Game: When a team bids and completes one or more contracts that score a total of at least 100 points, a game has been completed and won. When one team has won two games, a rubber has been completed, and the team with the most total points scored during the rubber wins the rubber.

Gerber convention: An artificial bidding convention used by a team to explore the possibility of bidding up to (and completing) a slam contract, when the opening bid is no-trump. It is initiated with a bid of four clubs, which requests that the partner indicate by their response the number of aces they hold. It is also used in part to conserve bidding space.

Grand slam: A contract where your team contracts to win all thirteen tricks.

Hand: The portion of playing Bridge that begins with the dealing of the cards and ends with the scoring of the results from either the completion of a contract or the failure to complete the contract.

Heart: The second-highest suit in rank; the symbol for it is ♥.

Hold-up: Choosing not to play an ace or other face card when provided with an opportunity to do so.

Honor card: The four highest-value cards in any suit: ace, king, queen, and jack. Also referred to as face cards.

Honors: Bonus points awarded when one player holds four or give of the top cards in the trump suit (100 points or 150 points) or all four aces in a no-trump contract (150 points). These points are recorded above the horizontal line on the scoresheet and so do not count toward winning games, only toward winning the rubber.

Invitation: A bid that suggests that a team explore further bidding to the level needed to win a game contract or complete a slam contract.

Jacoby transfer: An artificial bid in response to an opening bid of one no-trump that communicates to your partner that you have five or more cards in a specific major suit and requests a response indicating support.

Jack: The fourth-ranking card in a suit, symbolized by J.

Jump-raise: A bid that raises the suit at least one level higher than a simple raise: three hearts after one heart. Such jumps usually show a long suit and extra strength in your hand.

Jump-shift: A jump-shift is a jump-raise that also changes suits (e.g., three diamonds after one heart). This signals a very powerful hand.

King: The second-highest-ranking card in a suit, symbolized by K.

Lead: The first card to be played on a trick. All three other players must then also play a card in clockwise order, in the same suit if they can.

Limited overcalling: An agreement worked out in advance between teammates guiding the circumstances under which overcalls will be made and at what bidding level they will be abandoned.

Loser: A card that cannot win a trick.

Major suit: Spades or hearts.

Make: To successfully complete a contract, as in "He made 4♠."

Michael's cue-bid: A type of artificial bid that is in the same suit bid by an opponent. For example, if you bid two hearts immediately after a bid of one heart by an opponent.

Minor suit: Diamonds or clubs.

Misdeal: When some mishap occurs during the dealing of the cards (e.g., too many cards dealt to one player, the deck is dropped mid deal, etc.).

Not vulnerable: A team is not vulnerable when they have not yet won a game during a rubber. When not vulnerable, the risks of a failed contract are lower.

No-trump: A contract for which no suit will be the trump suit. The only factor determining the winning of tricks in any suit will be the face value of the cards played in that suit.

Offensive points: Points scored as a result of completing contracts. These points are added to the scoresheet below the horizontal line and count toward the winning of games.

Opening bid: The first bid offered during an auction. The player who makes this bid is called the "opener."

Opening lead: This is the card that starts the first trick of the hand after the auction is over. The opening lead is played by the player to the immediate left of the declarer.

Overcall: A bid that is made after a bid has already been offered by an opponent. Overcalls must be higher on the hierarchy of bidding than the original bid.

Overtrick: A trick won above what is required to complete your contract. Points scored for overtricks are recorded above the horizontal line on the scoresheet and do not count toward the winning of games.

Overtrump: Winning a trick with a trump card by playing one that is of higher value than another trump card already played on that trick.

Partial game: Points scored for a completed contract that are less than the amount required to win a game (100 points).

Pass: A call that offers no bid or any other type of call.

Pass out: Four consecutive passes in an auction. After the fourth pass, the cards are reshuffled and dealt again.

Penalty card: This is a card played in error that is prematurely exposed to the players. It usually stays faceup on the table.

Penalty double: This is a call that challenges the bidding team, indicating that you believe they will not complete their contract. It also increases the penalty they will receive for an unsuccessful contract. It is usually made at a high level, after the opponents have reached their final contract.

Penalty: The score awarded to defenders when a normal, doubled, or redoubled contract has been unsuccessful.

Pip: The face value of a card (e.g., ace, ten, four, three, etc.). Cards that are not face cards are also called spot cards.

Preemptive bid: A high-risk bid that shuts off bidding space from opponents so as to prevent them from winning an auction and/or a rubber. Usually made with a long suit but not a lot of face-card points, particularly outside the long suit. Also can be a sacrifice.

Promoting: Making one or more cards into potential winners by forcing out higher-value cards on earlier tricks.

Queen: The third-ranking face card in a suit, symbolized by a Q.

Raise: A bid that indicates support for your partner's suit. For example, bidding two clubs after your partner opens at one club.

Redouble: A possible response to a penalty double challenge by your opponents. If you then complete the doubled contract, the points scored by your team toward the game are multiplied by four. If you do not complete your contract, the penalty points scored by your opponents are multiplied by four.

Responder: The partner of a player who has made a bid or takeout double.

Rubber: A Bridge match consisting of at least two games, and no more than three. The rubber is over when one team has won two games, but the winner of the rubber is the team that scored the most total points during the rubber.

Ruff: Winning a trick with a trump card when you are not able to follow suit.

Rule of 11: A mathematical calculation based on the assumption that the player who led did so with the fourth-highest value card in that suit. It allows players to determine how many cards higher than the led card are held in the hands of other players based on the value of the card that was led.

Rule of 20: General rule for opening bids, specifying that if the face-card points and the length of the two longest suits are equivalent to at least 20, an opening bid can be made even with cards worth fewer than 13 total points.

Sacrifice: An intentional unrealistic bid, expecting to be doubled, with the hope that the penalty suffered by the failure will be less than the value of the completed doubled contract for your opponents.

Second hand: The player to the immediate left of the player who leads and the next player to play a card on a trick.

Sequence: Two or more cards in order: K-Q, J-10, etc.

Set: To prevent your opponents from completing their contract.

Short suits: Suits with zero, one, or two cards.

Signaling: Messages sent between partners during the play of a Bridge hand to communicate information with the cards led, played on tricks, or discarded.

Sign-off: A bid that reaches the level necessary to win a game and communicates to your partner to not bid up any further (e.g., four spades or three no-trump).

Singleton: One card in a specific suit.

Slam: A contract requiring the declarer to win either twelve tricks (small slam) or thirteen tricks (grand slam).

Small slam – A contract to win twelve tricks.

Spade: The highest-ranking suit, symbolized by ♠.

Stayman convention: Used after a 1NT or 2NT opening through which the players can determine whether the opener has a four-card major.

Stopper: A card in a suit that is sufficient to keep the opponents from winning many tricks in that suit in succession. Examples are the ace, king, queen, and jack of a suit.

Strength: An assessment of the worth of a hand of cards based on the total number of face-card points and distribution points in the hand.

Suit: One of the four groups of cards in a deck: spades, hearts, diamonds, and clubs.

Suit length: The quantity of cards held in a particular suit, either individually, or between partners.

Suit-preference signals: Messages sent between partners indicating strength or lack of strength in particular suits.

Sure winners: Cards held that would be certain to win tricks when played, without the need to establish them. For example, the ace and king of the trump suit are certain winners if they are both held in the same hand.

Takeout double: An artificial call usually made at your first turn to bid, and after a low bid by your opponents. It requests that your partner respond by bidding at the next possible level in their longest suit.

Third hand: The third player to play a card on a trick after the lead.

Trick: A series of four cards played in succession, with one card played by each player, clockwise around the table. The highest card in the suit or the highest trump card wins the trick. The player who wins the trick will then lead for the next trick. There are thirteen tricks in a Bridge hand.

Trump suit: The suit that temporarily outranks all of the other suits for that hand or contract.

Unbalanced hand: Any hand of cards with voids, doubletons, singletons, and/or very long suits.

Unbid suit: Any suit not mentioned in the auction.

Under-leading: Leading with a low card in a suit in which you also hold the ace of that suit.

Undertrick: A trick you needed to win to complete a contact but lost.

Upside-down signals: Messages sent between partners during bridge play that are the reverse of standard signals. In other words, signals that discourage play in a particular suit by leading with (or playing) a high-value card and encourage play in that suit by leading with (or playing) a low value card.

Void: When there are no cards in a particular suit.

Vulnerable: Your team is vulnerable when you have won a game in a rubber. When your team is vulnerable, the penalties for failure to complete a contract are higher. Both teams can be vulnerable simultaneously.

Went down: Failed to complete a contract.

World Bridge Federation: An international organization of bridge players from all over the world, the purpose of which is to support and promote Bridge play worldwide.

Yarborough: This is a hand with no card higher than a nine.

THANK YOU!

Please leave us a review on Amazon.

Amazon reviews are very important to
our business and help other puzzle
lovers find our books.

Please go to this book on Amazon and
let us know your honest opinion.

It would mean the world to us. Thank
you!

Don't forget to sign up to our
VIP Newsletter to get all of our future
releases absolutely free!
www.gamenest.org/free

Made in the USA
Las Vegas, NV
11 October 2023

78966608R00118